LIFE LESSONS from a TOTAL FAILURE

M.J. DOUGHERTY

the
hodge podge house

Life Lessons from a Total Failure

M.J. Dougherty

Published by The Hodge Podge House Publishers, LLC
Los Angeles, CA

ISBN 978-0-9972864-3-4 Paperback
ISBN 978-0-9972864-1-0 Hard Cover
ISBN 978-0-9972864-2-7 eBook
Library of Congress Control Number: 2016901906

Printed in the United States of America

Edited by Andrew Rutledge, Jason Quist, Kim Husband

Publisher's note:

the
hodge podge house
publishers

The Hodge Podge House is very proud to present this book to our readers. Although we stand behind our authors, The Hodge Podge House is in no way liable for the content of this book as they are the author's words alone. The Hodge Podge House has no control over and assumes no responsibility for author or third party content.

For Karen-
All of this is because of you.

and

For Pete-
I wish everyone could be lucky
enough to have a Pete in their life.
What would I do without you?

CONTENTS

INTRODUCTION
"Up Next..."
The who, why and what.

L ife is hard. Not only is it hard, but trying to get it to turn out the way we want seems impossible most of the time. No matter how hard we plan, try, and hope, life often has plans for us that may be different from our own. For example, in my wildest dreams, I never thought I would write a book. Although I have a great fondness for books, I was never much of a writer; I was always more of a watcher. I grew up in a small town in a small house with my mom, dad, and older sister. Our little house was bordered by two highways and a few businesses, leading to most of my childhood taking place indoors with the only friends I had in my neighborhood: the ones on my TV.

Television was not just my entertainment growing up, it was an extension of who I was. I thought about life in relation to how it would play out on a sitcom. Oh, the sitcom! Without a doubt, my favorite programming genre. I spent hours watching reruns of

The Dick Van Dyke Show, Mary Tyler Moore, The Brady Bunch, and *Happy Days*, to name just a few. I would wait all week for Friday nights to tune in to ABC's "TGIF" for *Full House, Step by Step, Perfect Strangers*, and *Family Matters*. Add *Saved by the Bell, The Facts of Life, The Golden Girls*, and *The Cosby Show* into the mix, and that pretty much made up my childhood world.

My teenage life became much more social, but I certainly didn't stray from my love of TV. In fact, shows like *Friends* became part of my daily routine. I felt a sense of comfort and normality just hearing "I'll Be There for You" playing in the background of my life. In many ways, this obsession with the world I watched through the tube led to the feeling that my life played out as though I *was* a sitcom character. I was convinced that after a long, hard day's work of being omnipotent, God would kick his feet up and tune in to *The M.J. Show* to see what hijinks and drama unfolded that week.

And honestly, like clever weekly scripts, my life has always been a series of extreme highs and lows – without much middle ground. It wouldn't be out of the ordinary for me to win the grand prize from a raffle I didn't realize I entered on the same day I nearly died while walking under a tree struck by lightning (true story). In the course of one month, I could bounce my rent check, not know how I would pay my bills, and then get an unexpected bonus at work that brought me back into the black on the same day my utilities were about to be shut off. That's just how my life was. It was my normal, even though I knew how abnormal it was to others.

Looking back, my life has had years of extremely good times contrasted with horrifically tragic times. I was a self-proclaimed flake who flitted about in hopes of finding myself and some form of direction. I bounced from city to city, state to state, and country to country, all the while picturing an opening sequence featuring me finally getting a fresh start as the epic theme song to *The M.J. Show* played. I love a good theme song. I was always on the move, looking for that perfect place with perfect people where I could be my perfect self. What I learned, however, is that life does not play out like a sitcom, and a perfect life is only found on TV.

My actions, thinking, and issues, along with a healthy dose of fate, all contributed to my life looking progressively more like a melodrama rather than a comedy as I got older. I may have made mistakes and displayed poor judgment consistently through my teens and early twenties, but when you are that young, you have an incredible way of rationalizing your behavior and staying positive for the future.

I assumed that this constant feeling of tripping into each new day while keeping my fingers crossed that I wouldn't fall was just how life was supposed to be. I patiently waited for the day soft music would start playing in the background while someone gave me a heartfelt talk, à la Danny Tanner, telling me how everything was going to be okay and I would soon find happiness. Unfortunately, as the years rolled on, that never happened, and my ratings must have taken a sharp decline, because my story line was about to go to a much darker place than I had ever experienced or imagined. It may have made my life hell, but it made my life one hell of a story.

I think about this dark time in my life as my "made-for-TV movie" era. You know the type of movie I am talking about: the type that plays endlessly on Lifetime, starring actors like Robert Ulrich or Meredith Baxter Birney, and titled something ridiculous like *Fighting Destiny for the Ultimate Love of Self: The John Doe Story*. The ones so over the top and dramatic, nobody possibly believes they could happen, even when they are "based on a true story." Well, the period of my life I am about to share was just that type of story.

It isn't based on a true story. It *is* my story.

I know some people may read this and think, "Big whoop! It could have been much worse. You could be starving in Africa!" And believe me, I know this and appreciate what I have. I do realize now, though, that no matter how it seems to you, someone's journey, struggle, and pain, is as real and intense to them as that hunger is to the starving child with no food. Perspective is a powerful thing.

Understanding people's perspectives and the fact that we all struggle and fail is what led me to share my story. Although I felt for a long time that my struggles were singular and my mistakes were one of a kind, I've realized more and more that my failures connect me with people more than they divide. Whether it's a young adult desperately trying to fit in or an established, mature adult who feels trapped in life, we all have things about us we would like to change and issues that we struggle with.

I also realized that we have an urge to hide our

issues and mistakes, and we tend to feel a sense of shame for having them. Knowing that others have felt this shame and hurt is the real reason I wrote this book. I don't ever want people to think they are alone in their struggles because in some ways, we have all been there. In fact, the more I shared my struggles and issues, the more I felt liberated and healed from them. It is common to want to sweep problems under the rug, but that never really works out well for anyone. Learning how to accept and grow from the worst parts of our lives is the most important thing we can do for ourselves. As a bonus, when we start being real and honest with ourselves, people notice, and we start making an impact on those around us.

So that is why I decided to share the story of this crazy time in my life. I would have loved to call this story *The Facts of Life* or *Growing Pains*, as I feel this was the time in my life where I was forced to grow up and learn about who I really was and how I related to the world around me, but unfortunately these catchy titles were already taken. *The Wonder Years*? Definitely not. I had to reach deep and think about a title that would not only capture someone's attention but really describe how I thought about this time in my life back then. So without further ado, I invite you to settle in, grab some popcorn, and enjoy the transcript from my made-for-TV movie, *Life Lessons from a Total Failure: The M.J. Dougherty Story*.

CHAPTER 1
"Cheers"
Life is a journey.

W alking around the small room and seeing every barstool full, along with most of the tables, gave me such a feeling of pride. I would often stand back and gaze at the long, narrow room in disbelief that I, of all people, that boy who couldn't stay still, owned a bar. Up to this point, life had been such a whirlwind since leaving my parents' house at eighteen. I hadn't stayed in one country, let alone one city, for more than a year and a half. Now here I was, grown up, becoming stable, and returning to my roots.

I owned and operated The Wine Bar in Scranton, PA, and was playing my part in what the locals were calling the city's renaissance. In a million years, I never could have foreseen me moving back to Pennsylvania and opening a business, but somehow it just felt right. At 27 years old, and after years of crazy living, countless mistakes, and never-ending uncertainty, I was excited to embrace my new life here and proud to have accomplished such a feat at such a young age. Look out, world, M.J. Dougherty, entrepreneur, has taken the stage. Cue the theme song!

To fully appreciate my change in fortune, you just need to consider my life as it was only a few months earlier. I had been living with my best friend since high school, Nathan, in Summit County, Colorado. I moved to Colorado from Amsterdam at age 25 after finding out that Nathan had cancer. While abroad, Nathan had been emailing me telling me he needed to talk with me. I assumed he was getting engaged to his girlfriend at the time and called as soon as I got the chance. I never expected for him to inform me that he had Stage IV Hodgkin's Lymphoma. I was devastated. What made it worse for him though, was that his grandmother was also very sick at the time and his mom informed him he would have to move back to Pennsylvania as she couldn't take care of two people, in two states, at the same time. After talking to Nathan a bit more, I decided to move to the little mountain town of Frisco, where he was living, to help take care of him through his illness.

It had been a really trying time, as Nathan's cancer was aggressive, and he had to undergo lots of intense treatments, including chemotherapy, radiation, and ultimately a stem cell transplant. The responsibility I felt for his life was overwhelming due to the constant reminders from the doctors about how any germs or illness he came in contact with could kill him. I spent months working to pay the bills, cooking, cleaning, and driving to and from Denver for doctor appointments and medical procedures.

I was working at a bank locally as a teller and the job turned out to be more of an escape than a place of employment. So many days I would go into work and my boss, Alyssa, would call me into her office to see how I was doing, just to shut the door and let me cry for hours at a time. I was the only guy who worked in the branch and these women who I worked with were my therapy. Without them, and the lovely customers, I would have probably gone nuts. Thankfully, Colorado had amazing people to help me through this terrible time and I love them dearly for it.

Nathan finally started to recover and return to an independent lifestyle after about a year. By this time, I was physically and emotionally exhausted. Even my beloved bank friends couldn't help my anxiety and nerves. I often found myself planning trips out of Colorado and spending hours fantasizing about life after being a care giver. This time was also a very lonely time for me due to the fact that I was one of very few gay people in the town. Although I had great friends and was living with one of my best friends in the world, I still felt very lonely, but the last thing in the world I had energy for was a love life. Fate, on the other hand, had its own plans for me.

As there weren't gaggles of gays roaming the streets of Summit County, Colorado, the only place I had a chance to meet someone was online. I was very weary of the whole online thing and tended to chat with people, but never actually meet. After chatting with one guy for a few months, I finally agreed to meet with him, but only if he came to a restaurant by my house where I knew all the staff. I told Nathan of my plan and advised him to call the cops if I wasn't home in a few hours. As I walked to the restaurant I almost turned back many times thinking I was crazy for meeting a stranger from the internet. As I sat at the table waiting for this guy, and then watched him walk over, I was taken aback by the thoughts going through my head. As soon as this guy, Pete, sat down across from me and started talking, the first thing that went through my mind was, "Oh! There you are. Of course it's you."

For someone who didn't believe in past lives, I was blown away by how certain I was that I had known Pete before and how immediately comfortable I felt with him. When I got back to my apartment, Nathan jokingly stated he was starting to worry that I had been hacked up by my Internet date. When he asked how it went, I said, with certainty, "I met the guy I will spend the rest of my life with!" Not even a month later, he moved in, and we have been going strong ever since.

With Nathan healthy and this new love in my life, I wanted out of Colorado, as cancer consumed my entire association with this state. After lots of chats with Pete, we decided to move from Colorado to the East Coast. Our plan was to make a stopover in my hometown of Clarks Summit, PA, just outside of Scranton, for a few weeks to regroup. My family owned a lake house nearby where we were able to stay, and we planned to use this time to figure out our next move. I knew I wanted to be in New England, most likely the Boston area, but it was going to be a big jump, because we had no jobs and very little money saved. So a free place to stay, all while getting to spend time with my family and friends, seemed like the perfect situation.

Pete grew up in California and spent his adult life in Wyoming and Colorado. These places couldn't be more different from the intense green of Pennsylvania, and he seemed to really be taken by the rolling hills and endless trees. Northeastern Pennsylvania, or NEPA, as locals call it, has some really beautiful scenery, and I enjoyed taking Pete to all the different places that meant so much to me while growing up and living here. It occurred to me at one point, however, that although he was now familiar with my hometown and the countryside of NEPA, I hadn't shown him around downtown Scranton. I wasn't really sure that there was much left to see, as Scranton had steadily been in decline my whole life, but Pete is an architect and designer, and I figured I should at least take him to see the historical and beautiful buildings of the once-thriving city of coal and trains.

I had never really spent much time downtown as a kid. I only vividly remember one landmark: an old-fashioned department store, the Globe. To this day, people still talk about it like it closed yesterday instead of in 1994. My mom almost cries when reminiscing about it! As an adult, my activities were limited to either getting my favorite pizza from Pappas (always add bacon, trust me!) or dancing the night away with my friends at a bar called Flashbacks. Of all the places I have been around the world, there was nothing like a night out at Flashbacks. With vignettes depicting different decades hanging from the walls and a light-up disco floor, my friends and I would hit that place, have a few $5 Long Island Iced Teas and dance nonstop 'til the lights came on. That was the extent of my familiarity with downtown Scranton. I didn't promise to be a very good tour guide.

One cold fall Sunday, when I took Pete for a trip downtown to the courthouse square area, I expected to see nothing but empty storefronts and old, rundown, albeit beautiful buildings. Instead, I was shocked to see people walking around with coffees in their hands. Not just coffees either; these people were sipping lattes that they explained came from a little cafe that was *open on a weekend*. I was really shocked and impressed. Although I didn't know much about downtown, I was certain this was something new.

That was the beginning of the end of our plan to move to New England. Before I knew it, Pete had a job he loved at a local architecture firm, and I was opening The Wine Bar. This time was such a blur that I still look back and wonder how the hell I did it. It is amazing what you can do with the energy and optimism of your youth! It was a mixture of sweat, laughter, tears, frustration, and exhaustion, but the result, my own bar, was pretty fantastic. I guess it just shows you that you can make all the plans for your life that you want, but in the end, life will always have the last word. I certainly didn't mind, though. It was nice to be reconnecting to a place from which I had grown so detached.

It was First Friday in downtown Scranton on the particular night I perused the bar. First Friday is a monthly local event in which downtown businesses invite artists and musicians into their establishments and enjoy a significant increase in foot traffic in and out of their shops. It is a wonderful community event that promotes local artists and generates a lot of free publicity for downtown businesses. Most locations encourage foot traffic by accompanying their selected artist with some snacks and a few bottles of wine, which definitely ensures a successful event in NEPA.

From the day we opened, which was on a First Friday, we always participated in this event by having a local artist use our walls as gallery space to display their work. It was consistently the highest-earning night of the month for us and was a great way to tie in the community with my little business. I was very passionate about doing what I could to help the downtown thrive again. Fortunately, there were several other local business owners who were on the same page as me, and through trying to make a better community, I began making great friends and connections.

In addition to participating in events, I made it a point to keep my business local. It may not have been the smartest move financially for a new business venture, but I believed that it would eventually pay dividends. The businesses were loyal to each other and everyone seemed to cross-promote one another. On nights like this in particular, I knew that most of my new business was probably being sent here from another business in town. This was a great feeling and is what made Scranton so unique in my mind. Everyone was involved in everyone's business. Eventually, however, I would discover the drawbacks of this intimate arrangement.

I knew that the bar could definitely be doing better, but as I was paying all my bills, I felt content. My business sense wasn't top notch, but what I didn't know about the books, I made up for in my understanding of people. I really enjoyed interacting with all the different people I met, and I know that the success I had with the bar was directly related to the personal connections I made. I may not have known everyone by name, but I usually knew them at least by drink. I would often see someone in the mall and yell, "Hey, Chardonnay! What's up?" and receive a huge smile in return. This small attention to detail brought me some loyal customers and made me some great friends.

I really loved my customers. In fact, I would get so involved in conversations that, without fail, I ended up playing host more than bartender. I would talk to everyone who came in. Of course, I would tell them about the wines we were serving, but then we would chat about anything and everything. I found that I got to know a lot of people very intimately. This really appealed to me on an emotional level. I liked to think that I had a special connection with all those people, and we had more than a customer–bartender relationship. I didn't hesitate spending hours talking to people and helping them sort through their personal crises. It made me feel so good to connect with people.

Thankfully, I had a few excellent bartenders who

picked up my slack. They always did a great job staying on top of everyone, so I never had to worry about service. With them attending to the customers' needs, I just got to enjoy talking with people and being an entertainer of sorts. Every night was filled with new people, and new conversations shuffled in with returning faces and continuing sagas – this really seemed to be the perfect job for me.

Like every Friday and Saturday night, we had our amazing piano player and singer, Ian James, come in and take requests after the First Friday artist was finished. As Ian started singing, his wife Karen sat at the end of the bar to start an evening of chatter among all the bartenders, Pete, and me. If for no other reason, meeting Karen and Ian and having them become part of my life was reason enough to be glad to have opened the bar.

As the evening died down and Ian cued the end of the night by playing the *Cheers* theme song, the real fun began. Some of our regular customers, who were now friends, along with Pete, Karen, Ian, and me, would remain after we closed to the public and stay til the wee hours of the morning talking, singing, and dancing on the bar. This was without a doubt the best part of owning my own bar, to be honest. So much fun was had by so many on our "lock-in" nights.

Karen and Pete were both originally from California, and they loved swapping stories and reminiscing in the midst of all these Pennsylvania townies. Karen had worked in Los Angeles for many years as a wardrobe person on various TV shows and movies. It was fascinating to hear her stories, and sitting in PA, as the snow was falling, it almost seemed unreal.

While I went through the receipts of the night, Karen pulled out a book of Polaroids from her purse containing different celebrities she had photographed while getting fittings. (This isn't a weird thing, by the way, it is what wardrobe people do to remember exactly what is worn by an actor for each individual scene.) Of course, I thought this was just the coolest thing ever. It was so unbelievable to me that I now had this friend, sitting in my bar, who used to work in Hollywood, but the pictures of various major celebrities in their wardrobe proved it.

At one point during that late, lock-in night, I started looking through Karen's photos again, and I was so impressed that she was able to do something so cool. I loved owning a bar, but to me her work was *really* exciting. I could only imagine what it would be like to work on a set in Hollywood with celebrities flitting about, crew members buzzing around you, and hearing the director shouting out orders. It seemed like a fantasy world that normal people didn't actually work in, but I was looking at proof that normal people did. I had a thought: in my next life, I want to do that. But for that night, I mentally returned to my bar, content with what I had.

When I went to give the photos back to Karen, she told me the story of how she became a wardrobe person. She was at a yard sale at a really cool house in South Pasadena, and while she was getting overly excited about some trinkets, as she tended to do, she started talking to the lady who owned the house. As they chatted, Karen expressed interest in clothes and fashion. This woman then told Karen that she worked in the wardrobe department for a studio. Before she knew it, they were exchanging info, and Karen was walking onto her first set, working wardrobe. She worked in wardrobe for a decade and had a love/hate relationship with it, but when she talked about it, I could tell she was proud of the work she had done.

As Karen put the photos back into her enormous purse, she said something so casually that has stuck in my head ever since. I was going on about how cool it was that she had worked in Hollywood and how amazing it was that she got to have these experiences. It was so foreign to me, and not something I thought real people got to do. As I continued to gush, she said with a wave of her hand, "Sometimes the best things in life just kinda happen!" That night in Scranton, in my bar, with these friends, I definitely believed that.

CHAPTER 2
"The Newlywed Game"
It's OK to keep things simple.

As the months rolled by, things went on pretty much the same since the bar opened. Slow weeks, busy weekends, and the bonus of holidays and private parties in between. In addition to First Friday, we liked to make sure we did something special for every holiday or special day we could identify. St. Patrick's Day, or "Parade Day" as it is known in Scranton, is one of the most important days on a Scrantonian's calendar, and we made sure the bar, like all the other bars in Scranton, was ready for a party. We also celebrated Mardi Gras, 4th of July, Halloween, Thanksgiving, Christmas, New Years, and even Election Day.

We also loved having themed nights, such as "'80's Night," where all the bartenders wore Members Only jackets, complimented with teased or crimped hair, and excessive make-up. Karen killed it that night, looking like Madonna right off the set of *Desperately Seeking Susan*, gloves and all. For our "Back in the Day" night, our friend Tony walked in dressed so perfectly in '70's attire that we had no idea who he was. This was how it went in the bar; we may not have been the busiest place, but we definitely had some major fun! I tried to think of as many ways as I could to get customers into the bar and keep things fresh.

Since the weekdays were slow, on the weekends I was always doing math in my head, calculating what I thought we would make for the weekend, including how much the bartenders would take home. It was really important to me that my bartenders made some decent money, as they were irreplaceable in my eyes. They all worked really hard and were very special to me. When we did a few thousand dollars in sales in a weekend, I knew it would cover all my bills, and I would relax. This was my routine for more than a year.

We were closed on Sundays, and that meant Pete and I both had one day off together. We often found ourselves killing time at our favorite bar and restaurant in Scranton, The Irish Bar, to unplug from our routine. We would spend the whole day hanging out with the bartenders, Meg and Brittney, along with whatever other staff and customers might roll in. Meg and I became fast friends the day I came in with a measuring tape and asked if I could come behind the bar and measure the sink. With an amused look, Meg gave me permission, and as I was measuring various items behind the bar, I introduced myself and explained why I wanted to do such a thing. Meg turned out to be a great help while I was opening the bar. She knew the bar business inside and out.

One Sunday, we were all chatting as usual, and the conversation turned to marriage and age. The concept of being 30 and unmarried was discussed, and it seemed to be a very touchy subject for some of the people here. The way they talked, it was as if there was something psychologically wrong with you if you weren't married and settled in life by 30. The conversation continued about how difficult relationships can be, and how so many people seem to be marrying just for the sake of having a wedding and not much for the actual relationship. This set off a spark in my brain.

I knew exactly what they were referring to. In my own life, I had watched many people get engaged and married who I knew weren't truly in love, or at least weren't suited for each other. Most were getting married because it was the next step in the progression of their lives and, frankly, some of those girls were simply getting married so they could finally be a bride. I had attended so many weddings where I had watched the whole, huge event unfold and was confident that the marriage would end in divorce. Pete and I had such a solid relationship. No matter what came our way, we seemed to be able to navigate it through communication and trust in each other. I found myself becoming annoyed that our relationship couldn't be celebrated in the same way as everyone else's, especially when I knew ours was real and would last.

Being gay, I was well aware of the fact that I couldn't *really* get married at the time, nor did I think it was something I had to do. I was very confident in the relationship I had with Pete, but I did also feel a need to make it more official. I started thinking about whether or not I would ever want a commitment ceremony, or something along those lines, to solidify me and Pete as a unit. I mean, we didn't need anything or anyone to tell us we were committed, but why shouldn't we get to have the same rite of passage as everyone else?

I obviously knew that I could not have a religious marriage ceremony performed by a priest or in a church, and I was completely fine with that. I just thought I should be allowed to have the legal equivalent, one that would give me the legal protection and benefits any married couple had. I used to panic thinking about what would happen if Pete got into a car accident and was injured. I was neither his family member nor his spouse, so I wouldn't be able to go see him if he ended up in the hospital or even get any information regarding his status. The thought of not being able to be there for the person I loved more than anything due to a lack of a piece of paper made me sick. I began to plan.

Not one to forego romantic traditions, I got a ring for Pete and shipped us off to Bethel Woods, NY (aka Woodstock), to see one of our favorite bands, the B-52s, play. When we first met, Pete had a very obscure song of theirs, "Topaz," on his iPod. "Topaz" happened to be one of my favorites, and I was impressed to see he had it. This, unofficially, became our song, so I thought a B-52s concert would be a great place to ask Pete to marry me. While there, I managed to talk our way backstage, and with a quick "You know I will always love you, right?" I slipped the ring on Pete's finger. That was how we got engaged. It was very simple and perfectly us.

It was more exciting than we had imagined to tell our friends that we decided to hold a marriage ceremony. Everyone seemed very excited for us and very supportive. They really understood why we wanted to do it. As my lifelong friend Amie pointed out, "you have to go to everyone else's crap, you should be able to have something of your own!" In one simple statement, she hit the nail on the head for so many of my own thoughts and feelings.

Karen and Ian had recently moved back to California, and when I told Karen about our decision, she quickly pointed out that gay marriage was legal in the state. We all agreed California would be the perfect place for us to take our next step, and Pete and I decided to marry there with whomever could join us.

My family was also very supportive. Most of my cousins were set to fly to California to celebrate, but many in my family, including my parents and sister, couldn't make the trip. Instead, my mother insisted on having a celebration in Scranton to celebrate with everyone, not just the few who could attend the actual event. So two events were now going to happen, the actual ceremony followed by a big Scranton party a week later.

Planning two events 3,000 miles apart occurring within a week of each other, all while running a business, was tough. Of course, Karen (being Karen) found this magical place in Laguna Beach that she thought would be the perfect spot for the wedding.

Within a few days, she had everything sorted out for my approval, down to the room where we would stay. Karen never even asked if I needed her to help. She is just one of those people who knew what needed to be done and did it. Talk about a one-in-a-million friend.

In typical M.J. style, we decided to go to California to get married, and then Proposition 8 passed, banning gay marriage in California (my ratings must have been slipping, and a plot twist was needed!). Although this was initially upsetting, we weren't too concerned, because we knew Prop 8 was being appealed and wouldn't hold up. Besides, even if we weren't going to get any type of legal recognition in California, it was important to me to officially recognize the evolution of our relationship in front of friends and family, so we continued forward as if nothing had changed.

The plan for California was simple and perfect. We would have a small ceremony with about 25 friends and family members, followed by a dinner on the rooftop of our hotel overlooking the ocean. It was simple and real, nothing too fancy or over the top. Good friends, my cousins, spectacular scenery, me and Pete. What more could you ask for? Well, Proposition 8 had, of course, *not* been overturned by the time we arrived, so the marriage wasn't legal... I guess we could have asked for that.

As we said our goodbyes to Karen and Ian, I wanted to take some time to really appreciate what a nice event we had. I was excited to fill everyone in on the past few days and the magic that was Laguna Beach. Unfortunately, there was no time for any of that. The minute we touched down back in Pennsylvania, party planning went into full swing.

I wish I could say that the event in Scranton was as easy and enjoyable as our time on the West Coast, but it definitely wasn't. It seemed like the party was starting to be planned by multiple people, some who we had asked to help and some that just inserted themselves. A whole lot of "you have tos" were being thrown at me on a daily basis, and every day it was becoming bigger and bigger. At first, I thought we should just hold it at the bar. After all, we owned the place, so why not just do something there? It was pointed out to me, though, that we would probably need more space for people, and if I had it there, I would end up running around hosting people. That was a very good point. I would feel as if I had to keep an eye on everyone in front of and behind the bar if it were at my place, so having it elsewhere made sense.

Instead, we decided to have our party at the oldest residence in Scranton, which was now used for events and a meeting space. It is a beautiful home, built in 1778, and the oldest home in the county. I liked the idea of making this a very Scranton wedding. The house just provided the rental space, so all events had to have companies and caterers bring everything in, which really didn't seem like a problem. In addition to the space in the house, we were going to have to get a tent to extend out back to accommodate everyone comfortably and make sure we had room for dancing.

Of course, I stayed true to form and made sure I was only patronizing businesses that were local and tried giving business to people that were friends or friends of friends. Between the food, the atmosphere, flowers, music, and the bar, it was going to be one great night. Everything seemed to be pretty much on track, except I couldn't get a firm number as to how many people were planning on attending. It seemed to be increasing on a daily basis.

A few days before the Scranton reception, my good friends Kathy and Siobhan arrived from Ireland. I had become friends with them a few years back when I was living in Galway, Ireland, where I moved on a whim at the age of 23. There is no place on this planet that means as much to me as Ireland, and Galway is like my home away from home. Over the years, whenever I would visit there and turn my phone on after touching down, my friends always had messages waiting for me wishing me a big welcome home. That is how Ireland is, no matter how long you've been gone, or how much you've changed, the place and its people are always ready to welcome you home. Having Kathy and Siobhan coming to my hometown, to celebrate our marriage, meant a lot to me because they were bringing a part of my soul with them. It was as if Ireland was sending me her blessing.

Speaking of blessings, there is another Irish girl who was part of our crew named Felicity. Although she couldn't make it to the wedding, Felicity had met Pete a while back and bringing Pete to meet her was more nerve wracking than introducing him to my parents. Okay, so that may not seem like a big deal, but you know those friends of yours who absolutely can't hide their true feelings from you and have no problem speaking their minds? Well, Felicity is one of those friends. Luckily, they hit it off instantly and I was able to breathe a sigh of relief. Pete: Officially Felicity approved. Thank God for that!

These girls really mean a lot to me and represent a special time in my life that was irreplaceable. They are the type of friends that you don't have to worry about or entertain, which was a good thing because as Kathy and Siobhan started to settle in for their visit, I had to put them to work. Catching up would have to come later as this now-massive party was just days away and lots needed to be done.

The fact that we were getting married had become quite a subject around town. I don't know how many gay couples had been married before us in Scranton, but I am pretty sure I was one of the first that was so vocal and in the public eye. It was great that so many people were interested in us and excited about the details, but it seemed like *everyone* knew about the party, and some people were not so subtly hinting for an invite. It even made a local paper when it was mentioned by one of the columnists as an aside.

I definitely felt a little weird about this and wondered if it was normal. This wasn't a frat party, after all; it was a wedding reception. Poor Pete is a fairly reserved guy, and he didn't love all the hoopla surrounding our little wedding in California, let alone a party this big. On the night before the party, he expressed his concern and dissatisfaction for how large this event had become. I assured him that there were going to be no surprises to him. He was aware of all who were coming and what was happening, so he would be fine. It wasn't like it was going to be a crazy spectacle or anything.

I was wrong – from start to finish, it *was* a spectacle. Right up to the last minute, we were running to get things ready. I had Kathy on a ladder hanging lights and Siobhan setting up tables around the venue. People were delivering items left and right, and of course, my tux didn't fit (the scene was straight out of a classic sitcom episode – very *I Love Lucy*). So much had been going on the past month, I didn't really have an idea of how the party was going to come together. With so many people involved and so many people coming, I was just keeping my fingers crossed that it would work out. When the time arrived, I was actually stunned that it all came together and at just how fantastic the whole place looked.

Then the guests started to arrive, and they continued to arrive and arrive some more. As we were greeting people at the door, there were several times I turned to Pete or vice versa and asked, "Did you invite him/her/them?" At one point there was a line along the porch, down the steps, and into the driveway just to get inside. It was absolutely crazy.

The party was a blur, to be honest. So many people, so much talking, and so much anxiety for it to all go well. Before we knew it, we had already gone an hour over the rented time, and we actually had to start kicking people out. One thing that definitely stands out in my memory was watching everyone leave. As a bar owner, I've seen a lot of drunk people in my day, but this stands out as the single largest crowd of stumbling people I've ever seen at one time. People definitely enjoyed themselves! By the time I dropped into bed, I was just glad it was all over.

What a whirlwind. What an experience. What a spectacle.

CHAPTER 3
"Family Ties"
You can't always be prepared.

With wedding events over, it was Thanksgiving week, and I still had the Irish girls at my house. Pete and I were hosting Thanksgiving for my family in the afternoon, and then we were all planning on going up to my aunt and uncle's house in the evening. I was excited to show the girls what Thanksgiving was all about, so I made sure they really got to experience my version of Thanksgiving, and it definitely ended up being "a Very M.J. Thanksgiving."

In the morning, first thing I did was put the Macy's Thanksgiving Day Parade on the television as I started prepping items in the kitchen. Pete and Siobhan were working on making sure the table was set just right, and Kathy, who is a chef, was helping in the kitchen with various things. In my mind, this was going to be a version of a *Friends* Thanksgiving episode, *The One with the Irish Thanksgiving,* that I would think back on fondly and remember as one of the best ever.

As my family arrived, I could almost hear the audience "awww-ing" as I hugged my adorable nieces in their holiday finest. My mom, my sister Erin, and Aunt Mary Eileen praised the beautifully set table while continually asking if they could help. In typical Thanksgiving style, the kitchen and dining room were a buzz with chatter from the girls, while the boys (my Dad and Brother-in-law Dave), were sitting on the couch watching TV. Pete was trying to make sure everyone was situated with drinks and trying his hardest to stay out of my way while I cooked.

Everything was going perfectly until I went to turn on the stove top to start the potatoes and realized my electric oven had picked that day to cook its last meal. Luckily, there was enough heat in the oven to cook the turkey long enough for that little thermometer to pop up, but all our sides that year were prepared via the microwave by a cool-thinking Kathy. All that planning for the perfect Thanksgiving and then the oven breaks. Typical!

After dinner, we all went up to my Aunt Renee and Uncle Jerry's house to meet up with the rest of the Dougherty family. The night couldn't have been better. It was the first time my whole family had been together in a very long time, and it was truly a Dougherty event, filled with food, drink, music, singing, and dancing. It was best summed up by my cousin Jennifer, who posted a status update on Facebook that said, "loves her entire family and wouldn't have it any other way!!!" When it was finally time to call it a night, everyone was either too stuffed to move, too tipsy to drive, or a bit of both, but we all (responsibly, of course) got ourselves home. I was exhausted.

To cap off my whirlwind month, that Saturday, I had my 10-year high school class reunion. I graduated with a remarkable group of people who were now spread throughout the country doing all sorts of interesting things. Thanks to social media, reunions today aren't as epic as they once were. We pretty much have an idea of where everyone is, what they are doing, and what has been going on in their lives since graduation. Still, I liked most of my graduating class, and I was happy to see so many familiar faces that weekend. For me, it was a perfect ending to what was, undoubtedly, the most memorable month of my life.

That week, after all the events were over, the turkey had been eaten, and my Irish girls were on their way home, it was finally time for me to get back to my life. I'd pretty much been in overdrive for the better part of a month, and when I got back into the bar and started looking at the state of the place, I saw some trouble.

November had been the worst month we had ever had, financially. Our weekday sales were similar to normal, but the big weekend crowds dried up completely. There was a major need for a huge liquor, beer, and wine order before this Friday, which was First Friday. The bar's heat bill, which was almost $1,000 this month due to unseasonably cold weather, was past due. I also had to pay rent, along with the usual monthly bills, and I realized there was no way I could cover all these expenses.

To say that I started to panic was an understatement. Luckily, I still had my party money, because I had only just received my bill for the catering and I hadn't paid for that or anything else party related yet. I decided I would use that money to settle the bar bills and get the inventory I needed. It really wouldn't be a big deal in the end since it was First Friday this week, and First Friday in December was historically one of our best nights of the year. My panic disappeared, and I moved forward, pushing any nagging doubts or worry out of my head by making my to-do lists for the things I needed to catch up on and complete.

On Friday, I got to the bar pretty early to get the beer delivery and to start putting away the alcohol order. I mindlessly put away different bottles, speculating about what the night would bring, until Shana, my bar manager, walked in. Shana is the best. A stunning beauty who can make the meanest cocktails. She was the perfect calming yin to my normally frazzled yang.

Shana started her usual routine of turning on the music, lighting the candles, putting out the flowers, displaying the menus, prepping fruit, and so on, and I went out to grab a few last-minute things we needed. First Friday was always so busy, and we liked to make sure we were as prepared as possible. I felt pretty good about the night. The Wine Bar was decorated for the holidays, so it looked amazing, and we had a great artist that month. It was going to be a great night, and everything was going to work out.

I had just come back from the bank with a bunch of change for the register and found Pete and Shana stocking beer into the coolers while throwing the empty boxes toward the back door. After emptying the change into the cash drawer, I started flattening the boxes to take them out back when I felt my phone vibrate. I grabbed a few boxes and started out the back toward the dumpster. When I reached into my pocket and pulled out my phone, the screen flashed, "Dad Cell." I immediately stopped in my tracks. My dad doesn't call me, nor does he talk on the phone. In fact, I didn't even know I had his cell phone number in my phone. I would guess that I had it saved from a time my mom needed me and called me from his phone. That's how little my father uses the phone!

I think everyone has those certain moments in life; times so burned into your memory you can remember every single aspect of what happened. The song "Paparazzi" by Lady Gaga was playing, I could hear Shana and Pete clinking the bottles into the cooler, I could smell the broken cardboard, and I was very cold standing behind the building when I answered the phone with a weary, "Hello?"

"Michael's dead," was all my father said.

"What?"

"Michael's dead, I need you to tell Jennifer and Jamie."

"Oh – Wait – What?"

"I have to go."

That was how I found out that my Uncle Michael had died.

As hard as it was to hear this news from my dad, I can't even imagine how hard it must have been for him to have to call and deliver news like that. After all, this was his younger brother.

My Uncle Michael was one of my father's four brothers. His youngest daughter, Jennifer, and I have been very close our whole lives. I was always with Jennifer, so I was always with Michael. Michael had divorced for Jennifer's mother years ago and lived in New Jersey, where he worked for Ocean Spray. Every other weekend, for as long as I can remember, he would drive from New Jersey to Clarks Summit to spend the weekend at my grandmother's with Jennifer, which meant that every other weekend, I saw him for at least one of the two days.

On those alternate weekends, Michael would consistently include me in whatever plans he was making or, more likely, whatever plans Jennifer was making. Michael took me to see all but a handful of the movies I saw as a kid. We would go bowling, miniature golfing, to the park, or sometimes we would just hang out at my grandparents' house, and he would make sure all the snacks and drinks we liked were on hand.

Along with my Aunt Sharon (my father and Michael's only sister) and cousin Alyssa (Sharon's daughter), many weekends also included making plans to go out to eat. At the time, Sharon and Michael used to drive me absolutely crazy when it came to making decisions, but now I think back on these times very fondly. I can picture them so clearly sitting at the kitchen table at my Gram's going back and forth with the same familiar exchange as to where we should go to eat. It went like this:

Michael: "Where do you want to go to eat?"

Sharon: "I don't know. What do you feel like?"
Michael: "I don't care. You decide."
Sharon: "I don't know. What do you want?"
Michael: "Sharon, I don't care. Just pick a place."
Sharon: "I don't know...I don't care either."
Michael: "How about pizza?"
Sharon: "Oh, ummm, I don't really feel like pizza!"

This exchange could go on for an hour. I am not joking. I used to get so frustrated that I would have to leave the room, but now it makes me laugh, and I would love more than anything to experience it one more time.

Besides our weekend fun, Michael also included me in his annual vacation to Myrtle Beach, South Carolina. Every year, Michael, Jennifer, Sharon, Uncle Pat, Alyssa, and I would make the long drive down to Myrtle Beach for a week of fun and disaster. Without fail, each year some kind of drama would unfold surrounding this trip. Problems often occurred before we even started, as we packed the cars in the driveway of our grandparents' house, and then again while we were actually in Myrtle Beach. From hurricanes to hospitalizations, there was always a story to tell when we got home.

It may not seem like this is the stuff great memories are made of, but they really were great times. We all had so much fun and, truth be told, none of these things would have happened without my Uncle Michael's generosity, devotion, and love for his family. He was the type of person who would take the time to know you and would think about what he could do to make you happy. As I got older, our relationship changed from that of an uncle and nephew to friends. In my twenties, I traveled a lot and lived abroad a few times. Michael was always excited to know where I was going and when he could book his ticket to come join me.

A great example of how Michael's brain worked involves the time I had decided to move to Ireland. While talking about my trip in my grandmother's house at Christmas, Michael made a very interesting observation. He realized that I was going to be in Ireland during the last season of *Friends*, which he knew was my favorite show of all time. He was so concerned that I wouldn't be able to watch the finale of the show that he pulled me aside and put $400 into my pocket to buy a television while I was there. He just wanted to make sure I didn't have to miss it. The fact that it probably wouldn't air over there at the same time as here was irrelevant to him; he wanted me to take the money anyway. He just wanted to do something special for me.

Michael met me while I traveled in Ireland, the UK, the Netherlands, and Belgium. On these trips, I got to talk with him a lot about his life. He would tell me about things in his past, mistakes he had made, times that made him really happy, and what he wanted for his future. We both loved history and would take forever getting through a certain area of a town or museum as we read every single placard. Then we would cap the day off with a good meal and a night at a pub, where we both would leave knowing half the bar by name. It was really fun for him, and I was happy to have him join me.

Michael came to visit for two weeks while I lived in Amsterdam. While he was there, I threw a party so he could meet my friends. The night started off calm enough, but by the end of the night, Michael got pretty drunk. My neighbor and good friend Brea happened to have a bunch of her friends visiting that weekend from her college. Michael started chatting up every girl in the room and playing his favorite tunes on my stereo, enlightening everyone with facts about why his favorite bands were the best bands in the world. To this day, Brea and her friends chuckle upon the mention of Uncle Michael. He definitely made a lasting impression.

The next morning, a very hungover Michael took me for breakfast, where he informed me that the previous night had been one of the best nights of his life. I remember thinking how odd that was, because to me, it wasn't anything special. Today, I don't care why it was one of his best nights; I am just glad to have been the one who made it happen.

Of all the men in my life, no one ever took more of an interest or encouraged me more than Michael. If I ever needed anything, I knew I could ask him, and he would help without question. I wouldn't even have to offer him an explanation; he would just help. He also just thought I was great. He would talk to my friends and tell them how much I meant to him and how he was so happy to have the relationship he did with me. He had recently been at my bar, and afterward, my bartenders told me how he went on and on about how proud he was of me. Now, my father had just told me that this man, who had been such an important figure in my life, was dead. He was 49 years old.

I walked out from the back room, looked at Pete, and told him the news. I told him I had to go and tell

Jennifer as well. This was not going to be easy. She was at work, and I understood why my Dad wanted me to tell her, as I was the closest in our family to her. Jennifer did not have the easiest childhood, and Michael was everything to her. I knew this was going to be something she would never recover from, and I wasn't wrong. To this day, Jennifer has never been the same.

I drove to the hospital where Jennifer worked and asked the lady at the information desk where I could find her boss. When I found him, I explained what had happened and he agreed that he would get her and bring her to me. I was standing in a room looking at an opened door that showed the hallway of the hospital. My heart was pounding out of my chest waiting for her. I couldn't believe I had to do this. As soon as she saw me, she started to smile, but then her face went white. She stopped in her tracks and said, "Is it my dad?" and I said "Yes." She pushed her back to the wall and wouldn't move. I asked her to come into the room to get her out of the hallway, but she just shook her head and said no. After I repeated myself a few times, she walked into the room, and I told her that her father had died.

It was as if she was a deflating balloon. She crumpled as I tried to catch her and direct her into a chair. Tears were rolling down her face, but she wasn't hysterical, just shaking and letting off a sound that I can only describe as the sound of someone in agony. To this day, the thought of that sound makes me sick to my stomach. My grief at this point was put on hold because I felt it was my responsibility to make sure Jennifer was OK.

Deaths in my life had become all too familiar by now. On my mother's side, I had lost two uncles and my grandmother, who I always say was practically my soul mate, over the years. Death on the Dougherty side though was happening like rapid fire, one after another. Over the next few days, as we planned Michael's funeral, our family started to feel the effects of another loss. Just a year earlier, my grandmother had died after a long battle with cancer, and we still were actively mourning the matriarch of our family whom we all loved so wholeheartedly.

Unfortunately, Michael's death wasn't the first tragic, unexpected loss for the Dougherty family either. In 1999, my Uncle Joey, the eldest of the siblings, passed away. Joey was a very kind and compassionate man who felt very deeply. He struggled with depression for years and, like so many people who don't get the help they need, turned to alcohol to ease the pain. After a long fight battling his demons, he finally gave up the fight and took his own life. It was something that altered our family forever. The pain, anger, and hurt that comes from a loss by suicide is something that leaves carnage wherever it touches. Suicide is truly a horrible thing.

As the reality of Michael's death started to settle in, I could see in everyone such emotional turmoil. No one was trying to hide their sadness or anger this time. We had been through too much for any one family to have to deal with and we were unraveling at the seams. I felt exhausted from what seemed like a never-ending string of tragedies when I went downstairs at my aunt and uncle's house and saw my Uncle Jerry.

I walked over to the bar, grabbed a glass, and poured myself a drink. I asked Jerry how he was doing and he said "all right" then asked how I was. I quickly launched into a babbling monologue of everything that I was thinking and feeling. I couldn't honestly tell you one thing I said except for the last line that came out of my mouth: "I just don't understand how anyone can deal with all of this stuff; it never seems to end."

Then Jerry paused for a second and replied, "Well, M.J., I have learned in life that you can't let the highs get too high or the lows get too low. You've got to learn to keep things in the middle."

Easier said than done for a person whose life is a series of highs and lows. I remember thinking that was a ridiculous and rather sad way of living life. Who would ever want to live that way? I thought it would be wrong to stifle one's feelings, especially the feelings that involved the high points of life. Well, it wouldn't be very long before I realized the wisest advice I ever received for how to live my life came from my Uncle Jerry.

CHAPTER 4
"Lost"
You can't check out of life.

Presumed myocardial infarction and cardio-pulmonary arrest from contributing factors of diabetes and hypertension – the official cause of Michael's death. To me, it seemed like a mind-boggling cause of death for a death that was mind boggling. In the days immediately after his death, I was so busy with my family and the funeral that I didn't really think about much else. While trying to think back on the actual events of those few days so I could write about it, I realized that I didn't remember much of anything. I called Jennifer, and we started talking, but her memory fades in and out as well. I do know this however: as the funeral events finished up, I fully checked out of life.

I stayed home, sleeping away most of my days. When I was up, I binge watched *Friends*, the show I used as my happy place, or *Grey's Anatomy*, because how can you not get lost in all the drama of Seattle Grace? I didn't leave the house, and I relied on Shana and Pete to keep things running at the bar. I ignored messages from people, often turning my phone off. I just remember feeling like it was cold outside, it was cold inside, and I couldn't deal with anything yet, so I didn't. It was almost Christmas now, and in my mind, I felt like the world could wait until after the holidays for me to rejoin it.

I found myself drinking even more than normal and being extra emotional. I often called Jennifer or Jamie, and we talked for hours about every detail of what had happened. Sometimes we just went to a bar or up to my Aunt Sharon's, and we all just sat, drank, and stewed in our grief. It was so dark and painful, and it was also completely unhealthy. I knew I had to start reeling myself in but wasn't quite ready yet.

Christmas came and went, and I can't even tell you one thing about what we did that year. We may have all gotten together, we may not have. It is a total blank. After the first of the year, I decided it was time for me to rejoin the land of the living and start to get some control and order back in my life. First thing, I knew I needed to finally settle the bills from the wedding party and see where I stood financially, both with the bar and at home.

I went down to the bar and, for the first time in weeks, I started looking through receipts and at the bank accounts. I had transferred a lot of money to the bar from our personal account (including money from Pete's paychecks at his architecture job) to cover everything while I was checked out, but I hadn't realized that for the past few weeks, no money was actually coming *in*. Up until November, I was always right on top of every deposit being made into the account, and I knew what was coming in and going out of all accounts on any given day. As I was looking through all the statements and receipts, I realized that not only was November a terrible month, December was even worse.

It was so bad that I almost assumed it had to be a mistake. Even on First Friday in December, one of the busiest nights of the year, we only made a couple hundred dollars. I was honestly shocked, although I shouldn't have been. I had been in the bar in the past two months, and it was always empty, plus, I had Shana telling me how dead it was while I was gone. I had myself convinced, though, that I was overlooking something or that there was just a mix-up of some sort.

Here was the reality, the bar normally would earn between $8,000 and $10,000 per month, which was all I needed to cover all my bills and give me enough to live on. In November, the total amount for the month was around $2,000. More than half of that was made the day before my class reunion, when lots of my classmates came down to check the place out. For December, at the close of the month, our grand total earnings were under $1000.

To make matters worse, Pete had put his notice in at his job in the summer and was finished as of December 31st. The bar had been doing well enough for him to help full time. We assumed that with the two of us focusing our efforts on the bar, we would be unstoppable. Now any other source of income we had was gone. I had taken pretty much every penny of Pete's and my personal money and put it in the bar account, thinking I would make it back in no time, and it would be no big deal. Well, I didn't ever make it back, and it turned out to be a huge deal. It was clear that I was in some major trouble.

Over the next few days, my mind never stopped jumping from scenario to scenario, trying to figure out how I was going to make the money I owed people and attempting to pinpoint what had happened to my business. I was well aware that I didn't run the most efficient business and that there were many things I could have done to build a more stable operation, but what I couldn't understand was how the business could have plummeted so drastically and so quickly.

It wasn't as if any dramatic change had happened. No major business or employer went belly up in town, I didn't take out all the booze and replace it with juice boxes, nor did I raise the price of a beer to that of a filet mignon. Even more puzzling is that in the previous year, November and December had been very strong months for the bar. I may have anticipated a little less business just because I wasn't around as much, but I didn't think it would be less than the normal average. This just made no sense to me at all.

My phone became my worst enemy and was now a constant source of anxiety. I was starting to get daily calls from people looking to get paid for the party, which was now six weeks behind me. The panic, shame, and embarrassment I felt every time the phone rang was so overwhelming that I honestly didn't know what to do. So I did the absolute worst thing in the world you could do when you owe someone money – I ignored all the calls. In fact, I went so far as to put some of the callers on my block list so their calls would go straight to voicemail. I just could not deal with the situation. I knew this was really a bad move, but in my mind, I kept thinking that as long as I figured this out and gave them their money along with an apology, it would all turn out OK. I just had to figure out how the hell I was going to do it.

Business for January was turning out to be worse than December. We were more than halfway through the month, and we hadn't had any customers in other than my friends. At this point, I wasn't even having Shana come in for most of her usual shifts because I couldn't afford to pay her and I was so embarrassed for what she already had to deal with. This was also the first time that I started bouncing checks from the bar, too. Truth be told, in my personal life, I have never been good with a checkbook, and I had bounced a lot of checks in my time, but with the bar, I was very good at making sure I always had them covered.

One Thursday in January, I was frantically running around, trying to scrape up enough money to pay the Internet bill because it had been shut off. I needed to get it turned back on that day so we could run credit cards for the weekend (assuming we had customers). While I was at the bank, Shana called to tell me that the guy from one of the beer distributors was there to inform me I had bounced their check.

A bar owner bouncing a check to purchase alcohol is a *very* big no-no in the state of Pennsylvania. Even if a bounced check is redeposited by the bank and cleared immediately, the state is notified, and they send a letter about it to your establishment. It also can cost you the ability to write future checks to pay for beer orders, which tended to be hundreds of dollars. It was not something I wanted to have to deal with and definitely not something I wanted Shana to have to be put in the middle of. It was clear that this was not getting better, but instead, with every day the bar was open, it was getting significantly worse.

I was at the point where I wanted to just run away screaming, because I was out of ideas. I was completely broke and desperately in need of money but had hardly anything coming in. Even more frustrating was that I felt I had a really great way of earning money with the bar but couldn't get it to make any. It was maddening to go through the routine of opening the bar, waiting around all night for customers, watching the time go by, and ultimately closing an empty bar. I knew I was going to go crazy if I didn't get to the bottom of this soon and fix whatever the problem was.

One day in late January, I was having lunch with my good friend Erin, and I finally got some missing pieces to my jumbled puzzle. Erin is practically a local celebrity in Scranton because she knows everyone and is one of the nicest, funniest people you will ever meet on this planet. She is also the type of person who doesn't beat around the bush and will call it as she sees it. As it happened, to be with me at this point in my life meant you had to patiently sit and listen as I freaked out about my latest catastrophe. I told her about a conversation Pete and I had earlier in the week in which we tried to figure out why the bar lost customers so suddenly.

Due to how fast and dramatically the business flopped, we wondered if maybe the fact that we had gotten married and the fact that it had been so open and public had rubbed people the wrong way. Maybe people thought it was unacceptable? Or maybe it just made them look at the bar in a different way. It was a wine bar owned by a gay man, but this bar was not a "gay bar." Was it gay friendly? Of course it was, as every place should be. We were friendly to any nice, respectful, paying customer. It is true that we had never had groups of straight men coming in to shoot the shit, but at least half our business came from straight couples coming in before and after dinner and for the entertainment, and the other half came from groups of women out on the town, young professionals, and yes, gay men. Until now, I had never really given it a thought.

When I mentioned this to Erin, however, that maybe us getting married pushed the bar over the line of gay-owned to gay bar, she quickly replied saying, "That's exactly what happened, but I didn't know how to tell you that."

I looked at her with a blank expression. "Oh wow, OK" was all I could say in reply. I felt numb from head to toe and felt like I was punched in the gut.

She explained how once we got married, the bar became "too gay," and guys just wouldn't go there anymore. Although the girls still liked the bar, guys just weren't going to be going to a gay bar for any reason. Unfortunately, what ended up happening was that without the guys even coming for a bit, neither did the girls. The bar then just dropped off the radar of places to go for the straight crowd of Scranton and became a "gay bar." Since we were not aware we were a gay bar and not marketing or catering to the very small gay crowd of Scranton, we really weren't getting that group's business, either.

At this point, even if I had embraced this as fact and dubbed it a "gay bar" or whatever needs to happen for a bar to be officially gay, there really wasn't enough of a gay crowd to sustain the bar or pull me out of the hole I was already in anyway. It wasn't that I didn't want to be a gay bar, but there already was a gay bar in Scranton. In fact, when I opened, there were two. At this time, in this town, that was all that was needed for that market. I certainly was never turning away any gay clientele, the same way I wasn't turning away any straight people. I didn't open a bar catering to anyone's sexual preferences; I opened up a bar because I really loved wine, and I really loved to socialize and interact with people.

I couldn't believe that my sexuality could be causing me to lose this place that I had put so much time, energy, and hope into. Could this really be enough of a reason to stop my old customers who I loved, like "Hey, Chardonnay!" from coming in? I mean, seriously, what did my ability to serve alcohol to patrons have to do with my love life? I also never hid the fact that I was gay, so why was it suddenly such a big deal? I lost everything just because I wanted to have the same milestone everyone else was entitled to? I felt like I was hit by a 2×4 and that the world I thought I had created for myself here had been a complete delusion.

Some people may not believe it, but I was born this

way. It is no different to me than if someone is born with green eyes versus brown/blue/hazel eyes. Green eyes may only make up 12% of the population, but it is a real eye color, and there isn't much to be done about changing it. In my mind, I lost my business because of something I couldn't change and because I was foolish enough to think I was just like everyone else. It was a tough pill to swallow.

Even if I wanted to pretend Erin didn't know what she was talking about, I knew she was right. I thought it had something to do with this deep down all along but didn't want to admit it to myself. The thought of this being true was too much for me to process. This was my home; these people were my people. My numbness was fading, and I felt a mix of betrayal, rage, and devastation. A part of me felt an urge to ask people how they could treat me this way, but another part of me wanted to burn the city to the ground. I had never felt such a dichotomy in my soul before.

Maybe I should have said, "screw it" right then and there and filed for bankruptcy at that moment, but I still believed I could save this downward spiral from reaching rock bottom and I didn't want to fail in this way. I went home and told Pete what Erin and I had talked about. Pete was less than surprised and seemed to be honestly shocked I hadn't figured it out yet. Pete didn't look at the area the same way I did. It wasn't his home, and he saw it in a much more realistic, honest light. After a long talk, we agreed there was only one thing that we could do to get ourselves out of our mess and hopefully rebound bigger and better. It was at this point that we decided that my beloved wine bar was going to have to shut its doors and, with the minimal amount of money possible, transform into something entirely new and different – a bar that would bring in the biggest crowds and have the broadest appeal possible all while wiping the gayness of The Wine Bar away. There was no more time to be checked out. I had to fix this and fix it now. Life, I'm checking back in.

CHAPTER 5
"Trading Spaces"
Out with the old and in with the new.

On January 29, 2010, great friends and a few loyal customers joined us for a last hurrah to mark the final night of The Wine Bar. As the evening drew to a close, I locked the doors to the bar with Pete and a select few friends still inside. I took down the sign, put brown paper up on the windows, and officially closed my first business. Thanks to amazing friends who were so supportive, we managed to make the night pretty memorable. Most of those friends with me that night I met as a result of their coming to the bar as customers. This was our version of *Cheers*, and now it was closed. My friends were all offering their words of support, remembering the great times we'd had, and even took the opportunity to lovingly mock me.

I never thought the bar was going to last forever, but right that second, I realized I wasn't prepared for it to be over so suddenly and under such circumstances. When you own a small business, it becomes a part of your life. Every day to me consisted of at least something having to do with the bar, just like every day I would brush my teeth or drink water, every day I worried about or worked on the bar. It just becomes part of you. So to be standing in the bar, knowing that tomorrow I would start ripping apart everything that made this place so special to me, I felt such a sense of loss. It was such a shame this beautiful bar (and it really was beautiful) had to go, just so I could wipe the slate clean and start over again.

Behind the granite and stainless steel bar, above all the displayed liquor bottles, hung five clocks that displayed time zones in various major wine regions around the globe. For me, I look back on this night and feel most sentimental for the moment when I took those clocks down. I had already decided that I wanted to give the clocks to a select few who were major cheerleaders for the bar, so as I took the clocks down, I handed them out, one by one.

It may seem like such a sappy gesture to be sentimental over clocks, but in my mind, the bar began and ended with those clocks. When I originally hung the clocks up, applied the silver lettering under each clock that displayed the wine region the time represented, and stepped around the bar to view them, it was the first time the bar, *my* wine bar, all came together for me. It felt so special. Now, as I took each clock down, I felt stinging failure. It was just as important a moment, but in a very different way.

I thought back to when I booked my first "Wine 101" class and how much fun I had teaching people about the history of wine and how to do a tasting. I thought about how much I loved to bring in new wines from different regions and introduce my customers to varietals and blends they'd never heard of before. I loved how we served every glass of red wine with dark chocolate chips and every glass of white wine with white chocolate chips.

I loved our cocktail menu! I had spent weeks on the cocktail menu for the bar so it was something interesting and unique. It had a mix of popular drinks from every decade dating back to the twenties, and I thought it was pretty spectacular. All that was over now. I never really had time for it to sink in or to appreciate it in its final days. The bar was already closed and parts were already stripped from its walls.

I really did feel as if I was in a sitcom that night. I felt like I was in my own version of that famous final episode of *The Mary Tyler Moore Show*, "The Last One." In this gold standard of sitcom finales, the six o'clock news gang at WJM-TV get the ax when the station gets a new manager. After the friends all spend some time together huddled and crying in the newsroom, they exit the place that meant so much to them, leaving Mary to take one last look and turn off the light. I wouldn't be M.J. if I hadn't done the exact same thing after everyone had left, with "You're Gonna Make It After All" playing in my head. I really hoped that theme song was right. I certainly had my doubts.

When I got home I went right to bed. I felt terrible. Even though it had been nice to spend the evening with friends and enjoy one final bash at the bar, I knew that whatever the next incarnation of the bar would be, it wouldn't be as personal to me as The Wine Bar had been. I laid there, thinking about how excited I was when I first thought to open The Wine Bar and all the things I was going to do with it. I felt so proud of myself and thankful to have the opportunity to do something so amazing. Now all I felt was a crushing sense of defeat. This was the start of many months of sleepless nights.

The next day, Pete and I immediately emptied the contents of the bar and took down anything that was The Wine Bar related. There was no time to be sentimental; everything had to go, and it had to go now. I also used this time to decide what, exactly, I was going to do for the new place. It may have seemed like I had jumped the gun a bit by closing before having a plan, but it was better to have been closed than to have been open and serving no customers. At least I could start getting us prepped for the transition. I had to act fast, though, as I still had bills way past due and people calling, wanting their money, but at least there was hope on the horizon.

One of the ideas Pete and I had discussed was turning the place into a cigar and cocktail lounge. We thought it might be a good fit for Scranton because at this time, smoking was still allowed in bars and most people in NEPA smoked. In the end, the idea was too niche, and niche was not what I needed. I needed something that everyone would like and would bring in the biggest crowds possible.

As Scranton is a very Irish town, and I am a very Irish guy, I seriously considered opening an Irish bar. After all, I had lived in Ireland, and I had worked in an Irish bar. I knew I could really do this bar justice, but there were a few major cons. First, there were already multiple Irish bars in downtown Scranton, all within a few blocks from us. In fact, The Irish Bar, the bar we loved, was just a half a block away. Another issue was money. If I was going to do an Irish bar, I could not do it half-assed. It would need a good budget to make sure everything was authentic – a place my Irish girls would approve of!

Finally, one day while moving tables around and clearing out paperwork at the bar, Pete came up with an idea. He and I were bundled up from head to toe but still freezing because we couldn't afford to run the heat, and also because it *was* freezing outside. We were talking about how horrible the weather was and how great it would be to be at the beach or on vacation right now.

Then Pete had his a-ha moment and said, "Let's do an island-themed bar, with a Tommy Bahama feel to it." I immediately knew that was the right direction. In an area like Scranton where, according to weather.com, the average annual sunny days number 70, a place that can even conjure an image of sun and warmth would be most welcomed.

From this idea, we chatted about many different forms the bar could take, but I finally made the decision on what I wanted. This new bar was going to be a very laid-back, beer- and cocktail-driven, colorful, fun establishment that would be in the style of a place that invokes images of fun, sun, and relaxation – a tiki bar. With a new light-blue, distressed bar and wooden tables, a stage for live music, and my favorite touch, little sand buckets to put drinks in, The Beach Bar was officially born.

Over the next few weeks, it was a race to do the work we needed to get done so we could be open for Scranton's biggest bar day of the year, Parade Day, the Saturday before St. Patrick's Day. Parade Day is no joke. According to Wikipedia, Scranton's Saint Patrick's Day Parade is the nation's fourth largest in attendance and second largest in per-capita attendance, in the country, drawing an estimated 150,000 people to its downtown, which is only about five blocks long and four blocks wide. Oh, and did I mention bars open at 9 a.m., and by noon all the bars are packed?

If I could be open for this day, I could possibly make enough money to put a dent in that significant hole that I was standing in. I heard that some of the bigger bars had made more than $100,000 on that day alone. The previous Parade Day, we didn't make too much because, since it was a wine bar, people didn't really think we would be participating. This year, though, I was planning on making sure people knew that St Patrick was on vacation at The Beach Bar! I felt like I had a good plan. Unfortunately, from here to there, I was going to have to borrow some money and involve more people to make this project come to fruition in the desired time frame.

The physical bar itself was mostly staying unchanged; it was just a matter of paint and major elbow grease. Where there had been a floor-to-almost-ceiling wine rack now was a place for a beer tap system that would connect to a walk-in cooler downstairs. The banquette that ran along the opposite side of the room, where we placed low tables with single chairs across from it, was ripped out and replaced with high-top wooden tables and stools. The lighting was also changed from a track system to pendant lamps to create a more casual setting. After weeks of no sleep, trying to scrape up just enough money to pay for materials and utilities, and still continually dodging the never-ending collection calls, everything was starting to come together.

About a week before we were set to open, my good friend Max arrived in Scranton to stay with me for a short time. Max and I had met a few years back in a hostel in Ireland and became friends while traveling in Europe together. When Pete and I had our ceremony in California, he attended and met my best friend Nathan's little sister, Megan, who I basically considered my little sister as well. Like something from a classic romantic novel, the two of them fell for each other over that weekend, and Max, living in Seattle, decided he was going to move to New York City to be with Megan. Before he hit NYC, though, he was going to hang for a bit in Scranton with me and help me with the bar. His timing couldn't have been better.

Max is one of those people who rarely gets his feathers ruffled. A bomb could have just gone off in his back yard and he would simply say, "Okay, so a bomb went off, let's just deal with it." That was definitely the type of influence I needed at that time! He was also a very handy guy who showed up with power tools and a tool belt, which I felt was definitely divine intervention. Speaking of divine intervention, I actually used to always refer to Max as Jesus because he is one of the most solid, real people you will ever meet and also happens to be a fisherman and a carpenter. (Side note: he is now a winemaker in Santa Barbara, too. So, in my mind, he is turning water into wine. Interesting.)

Something happened when Max came that I hadn't really anticipated. I found that when he asked me questions about what was going on and why we had closed the bar, I couldn't give him any straight answers. Normally I am an open book who often tends to overshare. I don't really know why I couldn't give him answers. It might have been because I was too ashamed, but I think it boiled down to pride. Pride, denial, and shame were the driving forces behind all my actions during this time, and because I still had some hope things would turn out okay, I tried not to let the whole story out.

At this point in the transition, I didn't know how it was all going to unfold. I had some hope, but it was barely clinging on. My life was a house of cards that was swaying forcefully, and this project was adding even more weight to the top. All I knew was that for me to get up every day, I needed to block out reality and the real, underlying causes of the current state of my life.

Fortunately, I didn't have too much time to think about it. There was too much to be done. So after Pete and I were done filling the bar with tchotchkes and Max finished climbing up ladders, drilling holes to hang TVs, beer signs, and artwork all over the place, it was time for us to get the bar opened. I definitely didn't feel like I was prepared or that the bar was ready, and in fact there were parts of the bar that were completely unfinished, but we had to start planning for Parade Day, which at this point was only a week away. Ready or not, I decided to open.

One full week before Parade Day, the new bar officially opened. There was no big grand opening, nor did I advertise it much. I wasn't even sure I wanted people to know yet, but I had to admit that the place really did look amazing. Getting it opened was a whirlwind, and it was one that didn't come without some additional risk and pressure.

Just to get to this point, I had to rely on some people who had done work for the bar before and who I cared about a lot to do work for me again but with only paying them the money to cover the materials. In an effort to dig myself out of debt, I had to dig myself even deeper into it first. The goal was to have a great Parade Day and pay them all. I was hopeful that this would be the answer to my troubles and that soon the nightmare of these last few months would all be behind me.

CHAPTER 6
"The Twilight Zone"
The definition of insanity.

T hat first week of The Beach Bar was all about planning Parade Day and getting inventory. I barely had enough beer and liquor for the week, let alone enough to accommodate the hopefully thousands that would come that weekend. Liquor was my main stress. I had to put my liquor order in and make sure I had enough but not so much that I couldn't sell it all. I also had to figure out how I was going to pay for it. Again, I felt like my life was robbing Peter to pay Paul.

I didn't have to worry about how I would stock up on beer, however, as the local beer companies had a policy for Parade Day. They would supply bars with as much beer as they wanted, then after the weekend, collect whatever beer wasn't sold and get a check for the actual amount used. This is just how big a day it was. Nobody could quite prepare for how much inventory was needed, so it was better to be overstocked than under. If nothing else, I knew we were going to have beer to sell for Parade Day, and that was definitely something to be positive about.

To my surprise, during that week, more than a few customers started coming in to check the place out. The reaction to the overall bar experience was very positive. I was really relieved. People seemed to like the vibe, and they understood the concept we were going for with the bar. Our large cocktail in a sand bucket was a big hit too! Even though we still didn't have a lot of inventory, we were just telling people that this was more of a soft opening and we weren't going to be officially up and running until Saturday.

I had made the decision that I wasn't going to let myself be too involved in the front-of-the-house operation of the bar this time. I figured that, whether people like me or not, it was better for me to stay behind the scenes and let Shana and Max work the front for now to make sure the bar didn't start off with any residual issues about whether it was a gay or straight bar. Again, it wasn't that I was against having a gay bar. I just knew that, financially, I could not get myself where I needed to be unless I had a really broad customer base. So, whether I was being paranoid or not, as soon as the bar opened, I stayed in the back room or sat down doing other things at a table toward the back of the bar.

The day before Parade Day, as I was excitedly preparing myself for my triumphant comeback, a group of guys came into the bar. I was sitting in the back of the room at a table going through some of the boxes of free merchandise the liquor and beer companies dropped off for me to hand out. It was amazing how much merchandise these companies would give the bars to hand out to people. There were hats, buttons, t-shirts, stickers, key chains, beads, etc., not to mention all the signs, garlands, banners, streamers, and other decorations hanging in the bar. As the decorations were already up, I was just sorting through the swag I would be handing out on Parade Day and making a schedule for the day.

Max was behind the bar, taking care of this group of guys, while Shana was walking between Max and helping a few other random customers. There were not many people in the bar, so it was quite easy to hear people's conversations, and I couldn't help but listen in on this conversation in particular:

Max: "Hey, gentlemen, how are you guys today?"

Guy 1: Fine.

Guy 2: Good.

Guy 3: (grunt)

Guy 4: Saw that you guys were open and just thought we would come in to check it out.

Then there was some small talk as Max let them know what was happening with the bar, what beer, wine, and liquor selections we had currently, and then he continued with informing them what we were planning for the future.

Max: Are you guys local?

Guy 2: Yeah, born and raised.

Guy 3: I am from New York but live here now. You?

Max: I am from Washington state.

Guy 1: What the hell brought you to Scranton?

Max: Well, my girlfriend is from here, and my buddy owns this bar.

Guy 4: How long has it been open for?

Max: Just a few days as The Beach Bar. It was a wine bar before.

Guy 3: Yeah, The Wine Bar, right?

Max: Yes, did you ever come in when it was The Wine Bar?

Guy 2: No, we never went. It was owned by a couple of fags.

I snapped my head up and looked over at the scene and could see that Max had tensed up in an almost defensive manner. Max came from an extremely liberal background and was not used to this type of attitude, and it was evident from the look on his face that he was completely thrown off guard. These guys were obviously so unaware that what they had said could be offensive in any way that they just continued with their conversation without missing a beat.

I shouldn't have been surprised, but even I couldn't believe what I had just heard. I didn't know these guys personally, but I knew who they were. One guy owned a business, and the family of another owned a very prominent business in town. Fags? A word like that has a lot of hate behind it and I was shocked, sickened, and pissed. Hearing that statement come out of that guy's mouth was surreal. You know how in movies or television shows, when something really significant happens, the character will be standing still and everything starts moving in slow motion around them? Well, that is exactly how I felt.

When life started returning to normal speed, I started feeling something new. I felt an overwhelming sense of reassurance and closure. I would even go as far as to say I had a sense of peace after hearing this. Over the past few months, I'd had more than enough proof that I had lost my business due to the fact that I was gay and got married. So even though I knew that logically, it had to be the case, deep down, I still thought that there had to be something else I was missing. I couldn't believe that was really it.

Sitting here now, listening to these guys' chatter at the bar, and hearing this guy so casually utter the line "it was owned by a couple of fags" erased any doubt I had. I guess me being quietly gay and having a nongay bar was acceptable for the majority of the straight crowd in Scranton at that time. Once I had tipped the scale to being too gay and too loud about it by getting married, however, the bar could no longer be anything but gay.

Closing The Wine Bar and flipping it had to happen so I could earn the money needed to get back on my feet and finally pay all those I owed. I'd thought a new business would have done enough to "shake the gay" from it. Now I had just realized something completely new. It was an Oprah a-ha moment, I guess. If people knew that this place was owned by gay guys, even if we weren't running it, it could end up being pegged as a gay bar again, and I might end up right back where I started. To reiterate, opening a gay bar at this time in Scranton would have been just a bad business venture. I needed to target the largest percentage of paying customers possible and make sure that was the crowd I was attracting if I hoped for a steady, profitable business downtown.

I guess I knew that with this new bar, I would have

to make sure I kept my personal life and, to an extent, myself in the background so I wouldn't slide the balance too far toward gay, as apparently I had before. What I understood now though, was that if I wanted this bar to really be successful, the best thing would be for me to not even be associated with it at all. To keep this bar successful and profitable, it would need other people running it and for me to stay quiet. This was infuriating.

What is the point of having a business, then? Why even own it? Besides, I still didn't even have the money to hire the people I would need to have The Beach Bar run on its own without me. From overhearing this conversation, I instantly made a new decision – I was going to get this place up and running, pay my bills, and sell the damn thing. I no longer wanted a part of it.

Parade Day finally came, and it was actually a really fun day. As I opened The Beach Bar in the morning, it looked like St. Patrick himself had thrown up all over a very cute tiki bar on a warm little island somewhere. I had been so upset by those guys' conversation that I didn't really expect to have fun, but with my friends, Pete, and our bar crew, I couldn't help but enjoy the day.

There was a steady flow of people throughout the day, but it definitely wasn't packed from wall to wall. Everyone was having a great time, however, and people really liked the bar. Even though I was well aware that the bar wouldn't be mine for much longer, I still took some major satisfaction from hearing how much people enjoyed it. Many people were even calling their friends to tell them to come to our place, as they were having too much fun to leave. That made me happy.

As the day went on, we had many different musicians and DJs come in. Every three hours or so, we had a new musician take the stage, which helped bring different crowds in to see the new act. This was both a good idea and a bad idea, though, as more musicians meant higher overhead for the day, even if they did bring in a new crowd. What I hadn't really anticipated was that the farther into the day we got, the more trashed the people were who came in. Having all-day music was not so necessary when people start drinking at nine a.m. By eight o'clock that night, the streets of downtown Scranton were filled with stumbling drunk people, and by this point, I knew it was time to close the doors for the day. Anyone who was coming in now shouldn't be served.

I wish I could say that the day was everything I had hoped it would be financially. At the end of the night, however, when the bar was closed, everything was cleaned up, and everyone was gone, I sat with a notebook and all the cash and receipts for the day next to me. In the notebook, I'd written down every penny I owed from the Scranton wedding party, what I owed from flipping the bar, and how much I'd spent in preparation for Parade Day. I had been up for almost 24 hours, and I was so tired, but I was still so hopeful that this was going to wipe all my problems away in a day. Truthfully, I knew enough just from observing during the day that there was no way we made enough for that miracle to happen, but maybe I would be surprised.

Here was how it all laid out that night. I was about

$7,000 in the hole from the wedding. Flipping the bar added another $4,000 of debt, and I had to settle the checks and money borrowed to pay for the inventory for Parade Day. For me to be completely out of debt, I needed to make more than $14,000 on Parade Day. I knew I didn't clear the $14,000, but I was hoping I came close. As I sorted all the bills and started adding up all the cash and credit card sales, the total for the day came to $5,000.

I put my head down on the bar and the tears just started pouring. My last hope for a semi-dignified return to the world was gone.

I had myself convinced that Parade Day was going to be the solution to all my problems. All the pressure from the work, sleepless nights, and emotional turmoil I endured dealing with everything surrounding my debts, disappointments, and the bar just started streaming down my face in the form of tears. What now? What the hell was I supposed to do now? Five thousand dollars wasn't even going to pay what I needed to cover the expenses for flipping the bar and the Parade Day inventory. Now I was even more in debt and would have even more people hounding me for money. I was worse off now than when I had started.

I sat at the bar, and my mind really started to race. How could I have gotten in so far over my head like this? I am not a stupid person. I should have known better. Why didn't I insist on paying deposits or bills up front when I had the money for the party? Why did I think it was okay to check out of my life for as long as I did when Michael died? I was now realizing the enormous effect my actions were having not just on me but on so many others around me. I was causing issues for people that were completely unnecessary, and all for what? I couldn't handle any of this. I was just too overwhelmed. I wanted out of that bar and out of it immediately.

CHAPTER 7
"What Would You Do?"
Never underestimate people.

After Parade Day, I was even more of a mess than usual. My self-pitying attitude was definitely turned up a few notches. I just couldn't understand why nothing was going right for me. I couldn't get myself to do much of anything unless it involved drinking or eating. I felt like my brain was in a race with itself to see how fast it could continually jump back and forth from one anxiety-producing thought to another. I didn't care how it happened, I just wanted out of my business and wanted out from under my debt. When I actually slept, I would have dreams that it was months in the future, and I worked at a bank. It would be payday and they would hand me a paycheck, and then I would go home. That was the whole dream, and to me, it was the best dream imaginable.

At first, I just wanted to close the bar doors and liquidate everything. In the state of Pennsylvania, a liquor license is considered to be like a piece of property. I knew that selling that alone would get me $25,000 to $35,000. Regrettably, I had a lien against the license because of my debt, but between selling the license and all the contents of the bar, I was still confident I could make enough to pay all my bills and walk away with this all behind me.

Unfortunately, when I shared this plan with my landlord, he said that he "wouldn't allow me to do that because it wouldn't be in his best interest." Crap. Not what I wanted to hear. Of course he would say that though. What landlord is going to want a shell of a room that was once a bar with no equipment and no license to run that business? He was also a lawyer, however, and he was the guy who facilitated my liquor license transfer, so for some reason, probably because my brain was too overwhelmed to think clearly, I actually thought that he meant I wasn't legally allowed to liquidate my assets, so I went to my plan B: finding a buyer.

The only reason I didn't want to sell the bar at first was strictly for the reason that it would be a long process, and that meant I couldn't pay my bills for even longer. Once all the paperwork is in to the state for a liquor license transfer, it can take several months for it to be approved. The thought of having to deal with this for a few more months made me want to run screaming for the hills, but it seemed as if I had no other choice. Luckily, I didn't have to look far for a buyer. Meg, from The Irish Bar, had been talking about having her own bar for as long as I had known her. She had been looking at potential places around the area to take over, but at this point in her life, she just couldn't afford it. When I decided to sell the bar, I knew this could be a great way for her to be able to have her dream come true and for me to get out of my nightmare. I approached Meg and discussed my idea about selling the bar to her.

She didn't take long to decide that she wanted it. The plan was to sell the bar to her, and on paper she would pay $30,000 for the liquor license and equipment. That was just enough for me to satisfy the lien against the license and would allow the transfer to go through. On the side, we made another agreement that she would then give me a monthly payment that I could use to pay my bills and start over with. This way I would still receive money for what the bar was actually worth (selling a turn-key bar with all equipment and liquor license for $30,000 would be straight-up asinine. The license itself was worth $30,000!) without her having to go in too far over her head in debt up front. It really was a win/win situation for us both. I felt like this situation was going to make some good out of something really bad.

We wrote up our personal agreement (that, of course, I had notarized), signed the paperwork for the state, and started making plans. Meg was looking to secure the money she needed to pay for the license, and I started figuring out what my next chapter was going to be. It was right at this time, when I thought I could have finally started to come up for air again, when all hell broke loose.

As everyone in Scranton knows, bars downtown make a fortune on Parade Day, so all the people I owed money to assumed I did, too. When I informed them that I did not and that I was, in fact, even more broke and now in the process of selling the bar to pay these bills and move on from this, everything escalated from bad to a living hell.

I was getting phone calls almost every hour from various numbers about different bills. Sometimes, when I answered, the person on the other line would simply say, "You better pay your bill if you know what is good for you." One time, when I stayed home from the bar because I couldn't deal with running into anyone who was going to harass me about money, a blocked caller left a voicemail for me that said, "Enjoying your night at home?" This was the end of me talking to anyone regarding any bills or debts. I also stopped answering any phone numbers I didn't personally know. Unfortunately, the phone wasn't the only way that the locals I owed were reaching out to find me.

After March, I had started getting legal actions taken against me in the form of civil judgments, and in a few cases where checks had bounced, people were prosecuting me criminally for fraud. This was truly horrifying. I had state constables coming to the bar, my home, and even to my parents' house to serve me paperwork for claims filed against me. I was so nervous that every time someone came to my house or through the door of the bar, I would freeze and hold my breath. I never knew what was going to happen next.

During this period, a friend of mine had asked if I would help her throw a party at the bar for her fiancé's 30th birthday. Even though I had all this going on, I was glad to do it. At this party, which I was throwing at cost, a friend of hers (to whom I happened to owe money) arrived. A few days earlier, I had been served with papers from the constable for a civil judgment that was filed against me for the $300-some dollars I owed her family's business. To be honest, I just flat out forgot about this particular bill. It was such a small amount, comparatively speaking, that I could have paid it at some point, but I was so focused on the major debts and the mess of my life that this bill slipped my mind. So, in the middle of this party (during which I was working, as it was a private event, and I thought I didn't have to worry about who was walking through the door), she walked behind the bar and told me that I needed to go to the cash drawer, take out the money I owed them, and give it to her right then. She then proceeded to tell me that her father and her brother were on their way down.

I was like a deer in headlights. My first thought was that I didn't even know if I had that much money in the cash drawer. I mean, I had *no* money. The second thing I thought was that I would feel so horrible if there was a scene with her and her father and brother, who apparently were ready to rough me up if I didn't comply, and I ruined this party for my friend who just wanted to do something nice for her fiancé. The next thing I knew, I was counting the money out of the drawer and apologizing profusely to this girl, telling her how sorry I was that I hadn't paid her and it came to this. I could see Pete looking at me and giving me a questioning look. Within a few minutes, she had her money, I had nothing left in the drawer and no way to make change for customers, and she forcefully stated that she would be drinking and not paying for anything while she was there. When Pete came over and asked what had happened, he was furious with me. A few other friends of ours came over and were also shocked at her behavior and mine. I was still just shocked that it happened.

My good old friend Erin was also there, and I do have to laugh when I think about what she said to this woman after: "Jesus! What were you going to do? Gotti him up?" All jokes aside, I think that is exactly what she was thinking. I mean, who does something like that? In retrospect, of all the poor decisions I made during this part of my life, this is the one that really shows me just how beat down I was at that point. If she did this to me now, for whatever reason, I would have kicked her crazy butt right out the door and/or called the police. Unfortunately, this event was just the first of several crazy encounters I had with my creditors during the time I was trying to sell the bar to Meg.

One night, another creditor came in to the bar, a bit intoxicated, with a man she claimed was her lawyer, who was also intoxicated. She sat with Pete and told him that she was there to discuss the debt I had with her. Now, Pete is a very smart guy. Exceptionally smart, actually. He isn't fooled easily, and he had a feeling this whole situation was not what the woman was representing it to be. He made sure he paid attention to everything that was happening. Other friends of ours were also there and observing the conversation. Pete took notes on everything that was discussed. Here are some of the notes from that conversation:

- "She stated that she and others have been

getting together and discussing M.J. and his debts."

- "She intended to file complaints to the state against the bar owned by M.J., and so would one other particular person. She said that they would file continuous complaints in an effort to ruin the liquor license transfer." (They did end up filing false complaints, which we were cleared for.)
- "She stated that it was important to them to make sure that M.J. would never be okay again."
- "She stated that she believed that he had done all of this on purpose." (Seriously?)
- "She said that she 'knows people in Scranton' and she has been keeping tabs on his life."

Pete explained in this conversation that trying to ruin the sale of the bar would ultimately just screw themselves, as that was the only chance for his debts to be paid. He then started to ask about the lawyer. He asked his name and if he could have his card so he could contact him about all this. The conversation abruptly stopped, and they said that was all they were going to say about the subject. Pete immediately went to the Internet and started searching the guy's name and never found a listing for him anywhere as a lawyer. This was clearly just an attempt to scare and threaten me.

Another incident occurred involving a company that installed some equipment for me in the bar during the transition. I had paid half of the bill but never made enough to pay off the rest. Although this company didn't have the long-term impact on my life some of my other creditors did, this company harassed me the most. Their employees would sit outside my bar and sometimes even my home, trying to intercept and confront me. As I was living my life like an ostrich, head stuck firmly in the sand, I didn't allow myself to be out in the world when I thought I could possibly be intercepted, so this tactic didn't work too well for them.

Instead, having been in the bar and knowing the various entrances of the buildings, they decided to take matters into their own hands. At some point, they went through an alternate entrance of the large building the bar was in and went down to the basement. Once they gained access to the basement, they were able to get into the bar, where they ripped apart the equipment they had installed and left. Though they never let on that anything had happened, they did let that bill stand and continued the campaign of harassment.

These were the types of things that I was dealing with during the sale. Collection calls from a call center are one thing, but how do you deal with harassment like this over debt? It was pressure that I had never encountered, and it made me paralyzed with anxiety. At this point, I couldn't really do anything. I didn't want to leave my house, I couldn't sleep, and I felt ashamed, embarrassed, and disgusted with myself. When it was just about me having to pay back debt and moving on from that, I felt I could get through that. Now, with such personal attacks, I didn't think I could see a light at the end of the tunnel.

I knew I could earn money and eventually pay all these bills off in a job. I knew I could start over and do something else with my life. What I didn't know how to do was face people. How was I ever going to be able to look people in the eye again? I mean, people were getting together to discuss how much they hated me and how awful a person they thought I was. These people, all of whom are interconnected to so many people in my life, are clearly telling people what a horrible, awful person I am, and who could blame them, right? I didn't pay my bills and that meant I was a bad human being.

How could I have done this to Pete? He had nothing to do with any of this. Even the whole wedding party was my idea and a result of me trying to please people in my life, and now it was causing his life to crumble as well. I knew it was a matter of time before all of my family found out, and how would they ever be able to look at me again? I knew that this had put two of my aunts in a horrible position, as they were closely connected to some people I owed money to. What would they think of me? Then there was the child inside me who wanted to cry thinking of the disappointment and embarrassment my mom would feel. How would she ever be able to be proud of me again?

"A barrel of a gun next to my temple...a barrel of a gun next to my temple...a barrel of a gun next to my temple!"

This became a mantra for me, and even the thought of that cold steel next to my skin brought a calm to my exhausted soul.

CHAPTER 8
"House of Cards"
It can happen to anyone.

I didn't have a gun, but I did have a bottle of Vicodin.

I had the Vicodin from when I'd had some dental work done, and I was pretty sure the bottle was almost full. I was well aware of how horrible suicide is for a family, as we had experienced the aftermath with the loss of Joey. When he committed suicide, I just couldn't fathom how he could do that to his family. I thought it was so selfish and just senseless. All he had to do was talk to any one of us, and we would have been there to help. Nothing could be that bad, right?

Now I got where his mind must have been. I was confident that I would never be able to recover from this mess, and there was no way out. Additionally, I was just exhausted from life. I felt it was all too much. I wonder if he felt the same way? Not only had I screwed up everything for myself, but I had taken so many people down with me. They didn't deserve that. Joey probably felt the same way too. I really understood now and I honestly felt it was the most sensible thing for me to do.

The past few months, I had been trying to keep my house of cards from falling, but to be honest, my whole life had been one big house of cards. At its base was a boy who knew he was different, who should be ashamed of himself, and should never let anyone see him for who he really was. I had been adding to this house with experiences that far outweighed what the unstable structure could handle. With the passing of each year, the weight was causing the house to shake and the base to crack, but now, with everything that was happening to me, the whole structure finally collapsed.

I was always aware that I had many issues, but I also always thought I would be okay in the end. I assumed that one day everything would come together, and I was going to be successful and happy. A sitcom rarely ends on a bad note-- no matter what craziness ensues. I was waiting for the resolution of my storyline, but where my life was at now was the complete opposite of anything I ever expected for me, and it was definitely not made for TV. It was my reality, and no matter what the outside influences had been, I was in this place because of my faults. I didn't have an ounce of energy left in me to try anymore. I couldn't be around for anyone else to realize my failures. I couldn't stand to feel any more hurt or shame. I was finally going to do the right thing.

On a Thursday, at the end of May, I had reached rock bottom and was ready to make the craziness of my life stop. I was going to kill myself. I wasn't going to make a huge production out of it. There would be no goodbyes, no notes, no getting my affairs in order. In fact, I was hoping I could get this over and done with without people actually even knowing what I had done.

I had been so stressed out, eating and drinking so much, that people were already very aware of how unhealthy I was. I'd gained so much weight that I hardly recognized myself. I'd been binge eating everything I could get my hands on, up to the point where I ended up covered in sweat with my heart pounding out of my chest. In a way, it had been my first, subconscious attempt at suicide. I had told Pete about my bingeing and how it was affecting me when I had been having one of those heart-pounding episodes, so I knew my poor health was definitely on his radar.

I had also looked up the side effects of Vicodin and discovered that it could cause hypertension and therefore could lead to a heart attack. My hope was that if I took the Vicodin and Pete just found me, it would be assumed I had a heart attack. Being 29 and having a heart attack might raise eyebrows, but being 29, weighing almost 350 pounds, facing bankruptcy, and having your world collapsing around you – that stress, I thought, would make it all seem plausible. I figured there was a very good chance that this all could be assumed to have caused my death and that no one would find out I'd killed myself.

I just didn't have any more fight left in me, and I didn't see any hope for getting out of this anytime soon. Meg still hadn't secured any financing for buying the bar, so I was no closer to getting my bills paid than I had been months ago. I had already shut my phone off permanently. Everyday brought more notices or summons. I sold my car, so we had no transportation. At the end of May, we had to be out of our apartment, and we had no place to go. For me, this was the only solution that made sense.

I no longer felt it was selfish to commit suicide. I felt that at this point, Pete would be able to move on with his life better if I succeeded. I knew he would be very upset, but the craziness of our lives was so overwhelming that this might be the out he needed to just pick up and leave with a clean break. Remember, we were not legally married, so my debt would die with me. Pete could just start over and not have the weight of my problems to deal with.

Most of my friends by this point were so sick of hearing about my issues that they were already distancing themselves from me, except for a small few. As for my family, what was one more death, really? My family would be fine. I spent most of my adult life living far away from everyone, and they all had their own lives and families that I wasn't really a part of anyway. I did feel pangs of guilt, but it was nothing compared to the sense of relief I felt when I thought that this would all be over soon.

That day, I waited until Pete did his normal routine and got himself ready to head to the bar. By this time, Pete, Shana, and Meg were mostly doing things at the bar. Due to my severe depression, I had effectively gone into permanent hiding. Once Pete was gone, I pulled out a ton of food and started cooking some of my favorite things. I opened a bottle of wine and drank it while I cooked. I put on some music and listened to a mix of some of my favorite songs.

The house was filled with my favorite smells, the wine tasted great, I started dancing around the kitchen, a bit buzzed now, and for the first time in recent memory, I felt free and content. When I finished cooking my food and my bottle of wine was empty, I poured myself a big whiskey drink, went over to the couch in the living room, and put on the TV to watch my comfort show, *Friends*, and shut off my thoughts.

After I had finished up my food, I was at that point of unbelievably full. Full to the point that it hurt and I was sweating. I was also very drunk and beginning to feel emotional and very self-pitying. I had taken all but three pills out of the bottle and left the bottle in the cabinet up in the bathroom. In my hand I had seventeen Vicodin pills. From what I had read, that was more than enough to accomplish the task at hand, and I was more than ready.

In my alcohol and food fog, I swallowed 17 pills down with one big glass of water, gagging a bit from the number of pills and the water hitting my overly full stomach. My last memory is lying down on the couch, snuggled up with my dog, Piper, and pulling the blanket over me with *Friends* playing in the background.

***

Freezing cold, face against a hard, wet surface, I woke up, trying to pry my eyes open and figure out exactly what was happening. Where am I? How did I get in here? Why am I lying like this? Why am I all wet?

My eyelids felt weighted shut. As I forced them open bit by bit, the light of the room stung my eyes. I felt extremely lightheaded and dizzy, even though I was lying down. I would have thought I was having an out-of-body experience, except for the small fact that every inch of me hurt like hell. After a few minutes, my eyes fully open, my brain no longer reeling, I realized I was on the bathroom floor in my house.

My body was in an odd, uncomfortable position, with my head toward the door and my legs toward the toilet. One leg was splayed out perpendicular to my body, while the other was wedged behind me, toward my back. From above, it must have looked like one of those chalk outlines you see of murder victims in old crime shows and movies.

The positioning of my body really didn't even faze me at first, though, because I was so cold I could barely breathe. I had to make a conscious effort to take deep breaths to feel like I was getting any air at all. Though I knew I was in my own house, the tile beneath me felt as cold and unforgiving as ice, and my body felt completely frozen in place. The liquid under me wasn't helping, either.

I wanted to get up, but my body just wouldn't respond. I would have panicked, but I could move my fingers and toes, so I knew I wasn't paralyzed. It seemed I was just so exhausted that not a muscle in my body could report for duty, so I had no choice but to continue to lie there. My head was very foggy, and my stomach hurt so bad it felt like I had been stabbed repeatedly with a pitchfork. I felt a mixture of nausea and acid in the pit of my stomach as well. My throat was so dry I could barely wet my lips.

I tilted my head up and could see two paws and a nose pressed under the crack of the bathroom door, and guilt washed over me as I realized that Piper was awaiting my return. I wondered how long she had been there. I really didn't like the thought of upsetting my dog. At that moment, a huge wave of emotion hit me, and I started crying.

My mind was already flooded with all my misery and self-loathing I was used to feeling, but now I also felt so physically horrible I didn't know what to do. When I finally got enough strength to push myself up, I realized that the liquid I was lying in was pools of vomit. It just seemed so appropriate. I was such a failure I couldn't even kill myself right. Instead of this being the end, it was just me having to figure out how to clean up another disgusting mess I'd made.

I hadn't counted on needing a suicide plan B, and I was confused as to why my attempt didn't work. Lying there wasn't doing me any good though, so I forced myself to get up. To walk, I had to practically hug the walls and fixtures. I needed to clean the vomit up from the floor as best I could and also get it off of me, so I climbed into the shower and turned the water on as I sat on the edge of the tub. I let the water hit me and simultaneously fall onto the bathroom floor. The water felt really good. It always amazes me how water can make you feel so peaceful. A nice, long shower can wipe away a long day's work, and the sound of water is so soothing. It was nice. When I was done, I took some old towels and started sopping up the water and vomit from the floor. I was really wishing I hadn't shoved so much food and drink in me.

When the bathroom was semi-cleaned up, I opened up the door to find a very stressed-out dog waiting for me. Her tail was between her legs, and she followed me very closely, never letting her side lose contact with my leg. I put on some shorts and a t-shirt and climbed into bed, where I held my stomach in such severe pain.

I *really* didn't know what I was supposed to do now. Is the medication still in me? Is it still going to work? Am I bleeding internally? I figured whatever was going to happen had to just unfold. I mean, it wasn't like I was going to go to the hospital and say, "Hey! I tried to kill myself, but I am not sure if it took or not. I feel horrible now, though. What should I do?" So, with Piper so close to me and watching me like a hawk, I just continued to hold my stomach, and I went to sleep.

The next few days for me are very hard to remember, but Pete filled in the gaps for me. He told me that I slept for almost three days. He didn't know what to think or what to do with me at that point. I hadn't told him what had actually happened immediately because I was too ashamed. When I did, he was very concerned, very upset, and very frustrated. Things had been so bad for so long, he just didn't know what the answer was.

He had been looking for jobs back out west, where he was from, and after this, he took control. We were moving to California, and we were going as fast as humanly possible. His decision, end of subject. I really didn't care what was happening and, truth be told, I was glad to have someone else take control of my life. Maybe he could do a better job with it then I had. It was time for a new director for this show.

CHAPTER 9
"Prison Break"
Embrace change.

As soon as I had recovered from the pain and exhaustion of the suicide attempt, my perspective changed dramatically. First and foremost, I was immediately regretting what I had done, and most importantly, I was glad it didn't work. I still don't know why it didn't work though. I have asked many pharmacists about this since then, but none seem to be able to give me any answers except, "Just wasn't your time, I guess." I think that the throwing up had something to do with it. Had I not stuffed myself with food and booze, I probably wouldn't have thrown it all up and wouldn't be here today. I am not going to say that I was now happy with life or that things were any better, but something about the aftermath made me appreciate things I had been taking for granted.

The whole time I was out of commission, in bed, not of much use to anyone, Pete was working tirelessly to try and move us away to a better life. He did not complain, and he wasn't angry with me; he just wanted a solution and wanted me to be okay. He had taken over dealing with the bulk of the debt collectors and facilitating the sale of the bar. Having someone in my life who cared about me so selflessly, as Pete did, was something I should have never lost sight of. If that isn't reason enough to appreciate your life, then I don't know what is.

It also may not seem like much to some people, but the love and support that my dog gave me through this experience, and during this whole time really amazed me. How is it that an animal can give itself so fully and honestly to another living creature? The unconditional love from a dog is really one of the most astounding and awe-inspiring things in the world to me.

With these glimmers of sunshine breaking through the clouds in my mind, I tried to do the best I could to keep myself positive and help us achieve our goal of moving. I wanted to continue to help get the bar sold and close that chapter on my life. Pete, on the other hand, wanted me out of Scranton *yesterday*. He knew that if I stayed any longer, the chances of me sliding back into a deeper depression were just going to grow. Meg had assured us that she had finally secured the money needed, and with all the paperwork already well under way, we let her unofficially take over the bar, and Pete and I decided that I should head to California immediately.

Here was our plan: Before I opened the bar, I had worked at a few banks in various positions and actually really liked it. I had been talking with Karen, who, again, was now living with Ian in Huntington

Beach, California, and I started applying for bank positions using her address as my home address. There were still too many loose ends to tie up before we could both leave, unfortunately, but Pete selflessly insisted on staying behind as he had less emotional attachment to the place than I did. I planned to drive out to Karen and Ian and crash at their place while looking for a job. Then, in a few weeks, when the bar was sold, Pete would join me, and we would be set to move on.

There were a few problems with this plan. The biggest one was that we didn't have a car, nor did we have any money. I would have flown, except Karen was emphatic about the necessity of a car in Southern California, so a car was priority one. I started putting anything of mine that I could possibly imagine people would want on Craigslist, and I managed to get a few hundred dollars that way. My cousin Jennifer had received some money from my Uncle Michael when he died, and she and I have always been the type that would help one another if we could when the other needed it. She said she would, of course, help if she could. It also felt like one more time that Uncle Michael was there for me.

I started looking at ads for every cheap car I could find that I thought might actually get me to California. I finally found a student at a local college who was selling her high school car, as her daddy had bought her a brand new car for college. It was an older-model purple Saturn, with under 100,000 miles on it, and it seemed pretty sturdy. She said she would take $700 for it. Sold.

My mom was working at a hotel in town, and Pete

and I had been staying there because she had gotten us a great weekly rate. We had enough to pay for a few weeks and then, hopefully, Pete would be right behind me with Piper once the bar was sold. On Tuesday, June 22, 2010, I said goodbye to Pete, Piper, and my mom in a lobby of a hotel in my hometown, Clarks Summit, PA, and I got on the road, headed toward California and a chance to start my life over.

When I was driving on the interstate that winds its way around the city of Scranton, a huge smile came across my face while tears began rolling down my cheeks. My life was never going to be the same as it had been before I lived in this city. I knew it was going to be a very long time before I would be able to get myself to come back to this place, if I ever did. I was also aware that there was still a lot that I had to deal with and that things were certainly not resolved yet. Mostly, though, I felt a sense of relief and freedom. I felt like I was going to be able to walk around, talk freely, and just live my life without a constant fear of harassment and shame. I had been a prisoner of my own life here, and now I was finally paroled. That was a great feeling.

I made sure to take a good, long look at the rolling green hills of Northeastern Pennsylvania as I drove. This was my home after all, and no matter what had happened, I hated how I was leaving here. Like a bad breakup or leaving a job that you once loved, the need to move on may have been necessary and good for you, but it did not negate all the good experiences you may have had. I still had my family, friends and so many people that really did support me here –

even when it wasn't easy to do so. Unfortunately, all that had happened in the past few months overshadowed that for me. I hoped that when it came to my relationship with NEPA, the old saying would hold true and that time would heal all wounds.

On my road trip to California, I stayed with some friends and family. I was really enjoying getting to see so many people I hadn't seen in quite a while. Also, none of these people had any connection to or knowledge of anything that had happened with me, my debts, and the bar in Scranton. With them, I could just relax and have fun. It was so refreshing and rewarding. It made me excited to really get the bar sold, get Pete out of there, and officially move on.

The day I got to California, even before seeing Karen and Ian, I went straight to the ocean to put my feet in the sand and see that ocean. Again, water. Nothing in this world can reset your soul like feeling the waves rushing over your feet. It was "June Gloom," as I was told by a local, but to me it was the most beautiful day I had ever seen. I was standing on a beach, 3,000 miles away from my problems, and I finally had something to look forward to.

After I had my soul-rejuvenating moment on the beach, I went to Karen and Ian's, where I was welcomed with a long hug and some dinner. We spent that night just chatting a bit and catching up on what was going on in their lives. It was so great to be sitting in their place and knowing that, sooner than later, Pete would be here and this would be part of our routine, just hanging out with Karen and Ian. It was going to be just like when things were good at The Wine Bar.

Ian was letting me use his cell phone to talk to Pete, and we were emailing back and forth. He was now bouncing between a few people's houses in Scranton with Piper in tow. I felt so bad that he had to be the one stuck there, but he seemed to be okay with it and assured me he felt better with me out of there. He also knew it wasn't going to be for much longer and was anxious for me to get my life started again.

I was trying my best to get things started, but if it hadn't been for Karen and Ian, I wouldn't have made any strides. Ian was working at a few hotels performing the piano show he had started at The Wine Bar and was doing really well for himself. Just about a week after I arrived, a one-bedroom apartment opened up in the complex where their apartment was. Being the absolutely beyond-generous and amazing friends they are, Karen and Ian gave me the money to get the apartment so we at least had a home of our own as a start.

I was over the moon. It had been months since I'd had my own place, and now I had a place in Huntington Beach, California, with eucalyptus trees outside my windows and a pool, tennis courts, and hot tub all right outside my door. This also was so encouraging for Pete. He at least knew that as soon as the bar transfer was finished, he had a place to go that was his own. No more couch surfing. It lit a fire under him to make sure everything was going as fast as possible with the bar sale so he could get himself into that hot tub!

I was applying for jobs on a daily basis to any place hiring. No job was beneath me. I applied for bank positions, to be a bartender, fast food restaurant worker, barista, anything, but I wasn't getting any interviews. This was new territory for me; I had always been able to get a job before. I went up and down Beach Boulevard in Huntington Beach and talked to every single manager of every single business that I could, and I was always told the same thing: that I either had to apply online or they weren't hiring at the time. I was starting to get really discouraged.

Finally, I was offered a group interview for a job with Wells Fargo for a banker position. I was so excited because I knew I could nail the interview and get the job. I had experience, I had great references from my old bank, and I actually really liked the job. I arrived for the interview, confident and ready to make a great impression.

I had never been on any type of interview like this before. I sat in a room with a group of candidates where they asked a series of questions and had us share different things about ourselves. I found it very odd but wasn't worried. I worked well with people, and I still felt that I was a strong candidate for the job. After an hour or two, they wrapped up the first part of the interview and told us that if we were selected to continue in the hiring process, we would be notified via email and would have another interview process pending a background check.

When I got back home, I felt good. I knew I nailed the interview and, although I was so excited to actually get a job, I was more excited about finally being able to do my part in helping make Pete's life a little less stressful when he got here. I wanted so badly to be able to make the transition for him smooth, relaxing, and fun. He more than deserved it. Over the next two days, I obsessively checked my email for a response, and then I finally got notification to log in to the Wells Fargo website, where a message was waiting for me.

I was so excited I failed logging in twice before finally taking a deep breath and successfully entering their portal. I clicked on the mail icon and read: "Thank you for your interest in the position. Unfortunately, you have not been selected to move forward in the interviewing process." I was crushed. I honestly couldn't understand why I wasn't even considered to move forward. I *always* get the job when I land an interview.

That night, I sat with Karen as we usually did, talking while we listened to Ian play at one of his shows. Karen had started getting an earful on a regular basis now about what had been going on in my life, and I was telling her how concerned I was that I couldn't seem to get hired anywhere. I didn't know if it was because I had been self-employed for the past three years or, if when applying online, my name was being kicked out due to background checks and all the judgments and financial issues I was having back in Scranton.

As we sat and talked, Karen bolted upright in her chair and started fluttering her hands as she did when she was really excited to say something.

"Oh my god! I have the best idea."

"OK, what?"

"Oh my god, it is so obvious!"

"What?"

"I can't believe I hadn't thought of this before! It is

just so perfect for you!"

"WHAT!?!?"

She then looked over at me and told me – not asked me if I was interested, but flat out told me, "You are going to do background work! I will take you up to Central Casting next week and you can be an extra!"

She continued telling me that in Los Angeles, instead of temping, a lot of people do background work in television and movies. The first thing you needed to do was to go to Central Casting in Burbank and register with them to be eligible for work. Then all you had to do was call the Central work line to see what shows or movies were casting. If you fit what was needed, you would submit yourself by calling the appropriate casting agent, and if you got through, you would be booked to work.

I could see that the wheels in her head were turning, and this made all the sense in the world to her. I asked her about whether they would run background checks or would want my work history, as that was my biggest concern these days. With a laugh, Karen informed me that Central Casting will literally take anyone. (I later found out that she was definitely not wrong about that.) As long as you can legally work in the country, they will book you for work.

I also wanted to know how the pay was and if work was steady. She said that work was feast or famine, and the pay was okay, but it was easy work. All you really had to do was show up to set on time, sit around and wait until you were needed, walk back and forth when instructed to, and not talk to the actors. You were also fed while on set and were able to go onto a lot of the Hollywood lots. I definitely thought it sounded fun, and it wasn't like I had any other options, so I figured I had nothing to lose.

The next week, Karen drove me up to Burbank. Registering to be a "background artist," as the Central Casting employee called it, was quite an experience. There was a line out the door, and the wait took forever. I filled out the packet of paperwork and listened to the orientation, which basically just told you all the things you could not do while on set, and then waited for my turn.

When I finally got to the table, actual registration only took a few minutes. The registration clerk entered my information, scanned my license, and told me to go into the next room for a picture. With that, I was technically employed and able to start submitting for background work. I didn't consider this to be really getting a job, but I was still excited. I figured if it helped put any money into my pocket, then I had nothing to complain about.

CHAPTER 10
"Access Hollywood"
Breaking out of your comfort zone.

A s soon as we got back to Huntington Beach, I rushed to the apartment and started working on getting myself booked for a job. I called the phone number provided and listened to the various things that they were casting for. My initial excitement faded very quickly after hearing the first two casting agents describe what they were looking for. Yeah, this didn't seem like it was going to be too promising for me. It went something like this:

"Hi, this is Jon casting for *90210*, looking for guys, 18 to-look-younger, extremely attractive, beach type, six pack, great body, if this is you please call..."

"Hi, this is Heather and I am looking for men with model-good looks to work a black-tie scene. Must have your own tux and be able to ballroom dance."

Are they freaking kidding me with this? Extremely

attractive? Model good looks? Must own your own tux??? As I listened, it did start to dawn on me that the fat, poor, desperate type was not exactly the desired look in Hollywood. I was going to give up right there and then when I heard a call for the show *Dexter*. They were looking for men, all ages and all types, for a large crowd scene. Well, I certainly hoped I could at least fit into that broad category.

I hung up the phone and called the number for the casting agent booking the show. I felt so nervous as I dialed. I had instructions that when the agent answered, you were supposed to just give them the last five digits of your Social Security number, but of course I was worrying about the details. Should I say "hello" first? Is it assumed you say "hi," give your name, and then the last five of my social? If I did it wrong, would they just hang up on me?

I didn't have to worry about what to do for too long, because the phone number was busy. I sighed a bit, relieved, and called back. I found out something important that day about working background: the numbers are always busy, and you have to be patient. It is a true Murphy's Law type of situation, because just when you are about to hang up and quit, you dial one last time and it rings. The agent barked:

"Last five?"

I gave her the last five digits of my social security number.

"Name?"

"M.J. Dougherty."

"OK, we are going to book you as an attendee. Please call this number [and she gave some number] after 8 p.m. for your call time, location, and wardrobe information."

Then she hung up.

That was it? Not even a "hello" was needed. These people meant business, and I liked it. My adrenaline was pumping. After weeks of looking for ways to earn some money, I was booked for my first job in my new life in California. I was going to be an "attendee" of something on the show *Dexter*!

I ran over to Karen's apartment to let her know. I was so excited, I was shaking. So was she. Obviously she was excited for me, but she was also excited for her. Karen really loved it when she was right, and she knew she was right with this one. I also was dying to call and tell Pete the exciting news. When I got a hold of him, he was pretty excited also, but I could tell from the tone of his voice he wasn't quite himself.

Things were starting to get a little harder for him, and the bouncing from house to house and dealing with the uncertain process of the bar sale was really taking its toll. He was still no closer to getting out of there than he had been when I left. Meg had not been very truthful about where she was at in acquiring financing, and we now knew she had no way of getting a loan. This was not good.

I felt terrible that I was away from all of that here in California and Pete was still stuck in PA, cleaning up my mess. The only helpful thing I knew to do was to make sure I got myself together so he would never have to live life like we did in Scranton again. So as I thought more about my first background job the next day and got more and more nervous, I knew I had to suck it up because I had to do it for Pete.

That night, I called the number that I had been

given promptly at 8 p.m. I was directed to be at the Four Seasons Hotel in Marina del Rey at five o'clock the next morning. I knew no buses could get me there in time so I asked Karen and Ian to take me and, of course, they did without hesitation. (My little car that had gotten me across the country had blown up in the desert. I had to run away from the car in the middle of nowhere while smoke was billowing out of it and hitchhike to get back to civilization. Seriously, you can't make this stuff up!)

Early the next morning, I was one of the first people to arrive at the Four Seasons. It was apparently going to be a big production day for *Dexter*, as the crew was set to film a scene where the main character goes to a convention to see a motivational speaker. There were going to be something like 300 background actors that day.

I felt like a foreigner in a country that spoke a different language. I had no idea what was going on, and I had no idea what I was supposed to do. I was definitely feeling a bit panicked, but I tried to remember that this was a big step toward getting my life back on track. This was also the first time that I remember my Uncle Jerry's advice really creeping into my head as my brain was starting to reel: "Don't let the highs be too high or the lows be too low; keep it in the middle, M.J." With that, I took a deep breath and calmly started looking for someone to advise me on what I should do.

I finally found a very nice production assistant to ask, who let me know they were running behind. I told her this was my first time doing background work, and she gave me a one-minute tutorial. She pointed to a table and told me to check in with another production assistant there, then go to wardrobe and get my clothes approved. "Then," she said, "sit, get breakfast, and wait." Sounded pretty much like what Karen said it would be, and for the first time that morning, I actually started to relax and enjoy the experience.

She wasn't kidding when she said sit and wait. A few hours had now passed, and the place had filled up with a ton of people. I was sitting quietly by myself at a table just people watching, listening to many of the background artists that were wanting to be seen and heard (and believe me, there are more than a few who are there to be the stars of the scene!). As I continued being entertained by the unbelievable stories and attitudes of people in the room, a lady came and tapped me on the shoulder. She asked me if I could come with her, so I did.

I followed her as she wound her way through the many tables and people in the big room they call "background holding." She took me into the hall of the hotel, where there was a group of about twenty people gathered and waiting for her. She then took us down some steps and into a room where a bunch of people were looking at equipment and chatting very seriously. I was completely lost and had absolutely no idea what this was about.

After a few moments, a man wearing a green shirt and an earpiece said that they needed a small role filled and wanted us to audition for the part. Say what now? Audition? The look on my face must have said it all, because the guy next to me said, "Not an actor, huh?" "Uh – no!" was all I got out. I thought I was just coming to eat some food, walk back and forth across a stage, and get a paycheck. What the hell does he mean, "audition?" My panic was starting to come back. Sorry, Uncle Jerry, but this was a time to panic in my mind.

He continued on to say that he needed all of us to act as if our favorite football team had just won the Super Bowl. Well, this was great – not only was I not an actor, but I haven't ever even watched the Super Bowl, other than for the halftime show and the commercials. In fact, when telling people this story, I often make the mistake of saying, "he needed all of us to act as if our favorite football team just won the WORLD SERIES!" That pretty much sums up how much knowledge I have of sporting events.

Realizing that I didn't have much of a choice, I started thinking back to the guys in college who would paint their chests, grunt, and semi-flex to show support for the teams they loved. So when we were all instructed to show our team enthusiasm as a group, I tried my best to channel those die-hard fans. I was very aware that I looked like a fool, especially as I looked around at everyone else doing their thing.

There was a man seated to the left of the guy in the green who was watching all of us. He gestured to the green-shirt man, and Mr. Green Shirt said he was going to go down the row now and have us do our reactions one by one. Now I really thought I was going to die. I started sweating and felt numb. This was NOT what I signed up for!

When he got to me, I did my best impersonation of a football fanatic reaction that I could remember seeing on ESPN (which I would have only seen because it was on while I was out at a bar). I yelled, "YEAH!" in the most guttural, masculine voice I could think of, all while shaking my fists in front of me, pounding on my chest, and gritting my teeth in a very stern way. Then I was done, and he continued to go down the line.

After a few minutes, they told everyone they could go, except for me. Mr. Green Shirt brought me over to the guy sitting in the chair. This man was the director, and he introduced himself and explained what they needed for the scene. In this opening scene, Dexter was going to be attending a motivational speaker's convention that was filled with die-hard fans. There would be voiceover discussing how uncomfortable Dexter was being in a room with people who were such fanatics, but at the same time how normal they made him feel, even though he was a serial killer.

He would then look toward this crazed superfan, who was to be covered in apparel and accessories with this motivational speaker's name and face on them. The crazed fan would look right back at Dexter and give an over-the-top expression of excitement and passion for the speaker, driving the point home that these attendees were nuts. I would be that crazed "superfan", and right now, I needed to go to wardrobe to get ready.

That day, not only did I get to experience what it was like to work on a set for the first time, but I was also able to meet Michael C. Hall (who played Dexter) and a few other cast members. I was being directed *by name* in this crowd of hundreds to make sure the shots were being set up right. For the rest of the day, people kept looking at me, thinking I was an actor. It was an incredible experience and definitely not what I had anticipated for my first day doing background.

By the end of that day, I felt something stirring deep inside me that I hadn't felt in a long time. It was a mixture of pride and real hope. Maybe this was a sign for what was to come for me here in California? Maybe I would have some more exciting, happy times in my life? Most importantly, maybe, just maybe, I might actually be able to put the issues of Scranton behind me? I mean, let's face it, when you are working on a TV show in beautiful Southern California, how can you dwell on anything from your past?

CHAPTER 11
"Deal or No Deal"
Don't put all your eggs in one basket.

I n the weeks that followed my day on *Dexter*, I continued doing more background jobs and found that I was really starting to love every minute of it. I worked on *The Middle*, *The Mentalist*, *Bones*, *House*, and *Glee*, to name a few shows, as well as a bunch of movies. Every time I was booked for something, I would get the biggest wave of excitement, but that excitement was nothing compared to how I felt the first time I ever saw myself on TV.

When the episode of *Dexter* aired, I found out because people started calling and texting me about it. I was really overjoyed. Okay, overjoyed is an understatement. When I saw the clip of me on that TV show, I was flipping out like the kids in those commercials for Disney World when they find out they're going. There was definitely some screaming and jumping up and down! Seeing myself, fat as I was, still brought out an excitement in me I have rarely ever felt before.

The icing on the cake was when I got the letter in the mail that said I was eligible to join the Screen Actors Guild a few months later. I was almost in disbelief. In just a few months, I got my SAG card and was considered a professional actor. I really felt that this might be something more than a temporary thing for me. A little inkling of a career in Hollywood started to pop into my brain, but I thought it was not acceptable to focus my energy on that. For now, it was a way to make money and to make things smoother for Pete when he arrived. I also felt it was important to make sure that my past was all squared away before making any real steps toward my new future. I wanted to make sure I had a line in the sand separating my pre-California life and now.

Working in Hollywood gave me a feeling of accomplishment, or at least the feeling like I could do something exciting with my life again. The feeling that I might be able to make my mom proud once more definitely started to seem like a goal within reach. I was definitely ready to start moving on with my life, but I was still quite a long way off from that happening. As much as I wanted to just pretend everything was all over with, it was pretty much impossible to do that, because Pete still hadn't left Scranton.

It had been more than three months, and Pete was losing his mind being stuck there, staying at people's houses, and not having any answers as to when he was going to get to leave. While Meg was in the process of getting the liquor license turned over to her name, she still couldn't secure the financing needed to pay for it. She had been giving us a lot of false reassurance about where she was in the process, but now we were seeing the truth. It seemed like we were going to have to cancel the whole sale, find someone else to buy the bar, and start all over again.

Although I was in California and finding some work, I had no permanent job and wasn't earning nearly enough money to live off of, let alone settle the bills in PA and get Pete out of there. Pete was starting to really resent the world, as he was stuck in Pennsylvania with no job, no home, and no money. To top it all off, the people who had threatened to report the bar to the state were now following through on their threat, and the bar received a visit from the Liquor Control Board. This nightmare was never going to end.

Just when I was about to crack, I learned that our landlord at the bar had agreed to cosign a loan for Meg so she could pay for the transfer of the bar. It seemed like this was the answer to all our prayers, or at least mine and Pete's, but it definitely wasn't. The landlord had agreed to cosign a loan for Meg so she had the money to fulfill the agreement that was made with the State of Pennsylvania for the sale of the bar and liquor license, in the sum of $30,000.

Unfortunately, he had agreed to do this on the condition that Meg did not pay me the monthly payment she had promised to pay until after the loan with him was paid off.

When I first decided to sell the bar, I knew how much I needed to clear all my debt. I would have had to either charge Meg for the cost of the whole amount of my debt up front, so I could settle my debt and the lien I had against the liquor license, or I could do an agreement between friends that would be just enough to settle the lien against the license, give her the bar to run so she could earn money, and then she could pay me monthly moving forward. I knew she wouldn't be able to come up with that type of financing to buy it outright, and I really wanted her to be able to have the bar. So the agreement between us for monthly payments was the best option. With that, I could start knocking out my bills month by month, and then finally make a few bucks back from the more than $150,000 I put into the bar myself.

Remember, in writing, Meg and I had our own notarized agreement that was separate from the state agreement stating that she would pay $30,000 to take ownership of the bar and then pay a monthly fee to me for five years. The paperwork for the state and the liquor license transfer showed the price of the bar had been set at $30,000. We needed to keep it reasonable so Meg could obtain financing and be able to pay the license transfer free and clear.

It was broken down on that paperwork that she would pay $15,000 for the liquor license and $15,000 for the contents of the bar. In a million years, I would have never agreed to sell the bar for a total of $30,000 when I paid $30,000 just for the liquor license alone. What would have been the point of that? I would have not been able to pay my bills, get Pete to CA, or make anything back from the hundreds of thousands of dollars I'd put into the place. I understood that this was just what I needed to get this process resolved legally and I had faith that it would all work out.

Now, there I stood in California, being told that I wasn't going to get any of those monthly payments from Meg. That meant that from the sale of my bar, I wouldn't get anything. No bills paid, no way for Pete to get here, nothing. When I called the landlord freaking out, he informed me that he had to look out for his best interest. By cosigning the loan for Meg, he was putting risk on himself and wanted that loan paid back first before she paid anything else.

When I informed him that I was counting on those monthly payments to help pay my debts and get back on my feet, he told me Meg would have a "moral obligation" to pay me eventually. When I called Meg in a panic, she told me I shouldn't worry about that, and although she wouldn't have money to pay right away, of course she would pay when she could and would never screw me.

In the end, I really didn't have much of a choice. What was I supposed to do, go back to Pennsylvania and start looking for a buyer all over again? My Uncle Jerry's voice was whispering in my ear, "don't let the highs be too high or the lows be too low!" Remembering to keep my emotions in the middle, I realized I still wanted Meg to have my bar, as she was my friend and I had worked so hard on it, and it had cost me so much. In the end, I would have hated the thought of it being stripped to nothing and have all traces of my accomplishment wiped out. At least knowing that Meg would have it meant that it would almost feel like a piece of it was still mine. I decided to believe her words and trust that she would pay me eventually and focus on the fact that it was just another bump in the road that I would get through.

After Meg finally got the loan and the transfer went through, all that $30,000 was taken by the lien I had against the license and the rest given to my landlord for back rent. I didn't get anything. I could deal with making no money off of this sale, but what was so hard is that now I still couldn't pay my debts, and there was no money for Pete to get himself out here. Sure, I knew that eventually I was supposed to get money from Meg, but that didn't help me now. I had more issues to deal with now than before, but at least I wasn't responsible for that bar anymore. That was one thing I was really grateful for.

Pete had, by now, completely lost his mind and was pretty much telling everyone who would listen exactly what he thought of Northeastern Pennsylvania and all who inhabited it (I would elaborate, but his thoughts at this point were nothing I should put in writing!). He didn't care what the reasons were; he felt we were screwed over in this transaction and had no problem vocalizing it. Unlike me, he didn't trust Meg, didn't consider her a friend, and thought she was nothing more than a con-artist playing everyone to get what she wanted. He had witnessed her and caught her in too many lies, too many times. He was furious.

Aside from his uncharacteristic anger, Pete, who was a life-long runner and outdoors enthusiast, had completely stopped running and was spending most of his time inside watching TV or drinking with the few remaining people he could tolerate. This was not the person he normally was, and I was so worried about him. I had to figure something out, so I started making calls and begging people for some help to get him out of there. I also encouraged Pete to tell people how he felt and show his emotion because that way people couldn't think it was just me overreacting.

Seeing Pete in this state was a shock to everyone. He was always so controlled and rational that I think when he finally snapped, people took notice. Pete started going into the bar telling everyone who would listen what had happened with the sale and just what he thought about it. Over the next few days, he managed to scrounge up enough money to get on the road and headed to California. With the little money I had earned and what he managed to scrounge up, Pete bought an old truck for just under a thousand dollars. He immediately packed the back with the few items we still owned, put Piper in the passenger seat, and pretty much floored it out of NEPA with no desire to ever return.

On November 3, 2010, more than four months after I left Pennsylvania, Pete and Piper pulled into the parking lot of our apartment complex in Huntington Beach, California. Seeing him through the windshield with Piper next to him made me so happy that I was shaking from head to toe. Piper was sitting up so straight looking out the windshield that she almost looked human, and Pete's smile was so big I could see it from down the road. I was so excited; I felt like a kid at Christmas. He was here, we were together, and even though things weren't all settled, right then, I didn't care. This was the moment I had waited for, and I was content.

CHAPTER 12
"Friends"
Wish less. Appreciate more.

It wasn't that my dreamed-up *The M.J. Show* was throwing additional plot twists into my life at this point, but that reality just began shaking up our day-to-day instead. We desperately tried to just enjoy life the first few weeks after Pete arrived, but we still had a lot of issues that needed to be dealt with. Although we were enjoying spending time with Karen and Ian, exploring the town, going to the beach, and frequenting our favorite place to hang, the library (it's free!), we were still utterly broke.

Background work began slowing, so Pete and I went to Los Angeles a lot to do audience work. Audience work is this horrible experience where you get treated like crap to sit in the crowd of a show and clap. We absolutely hated every minute of it, but it paid $8 an hour cash at the end of taping, and for two people who had no work, it was money well appreciated.

Pete was trying hard to get a job and was a little

frustrated at his lack of options. He sent his portfolio off to every architecture and design firm in Southern California, but the stagnant economy offered him little response. It was so hard for me to watch him suffering so much and knowing that this was all because of my poor decisions and my issues.

Between audience work and whatever background work I could find, we struggled to make enough money to pay our rent. There was no way I could even spare a dollar to the bills that were still haunting me from Scranton. With most of our work in LA, the cost of driving back and forth was also taking its toll. Our initial excitement to just be together and in California quickly wore off, and now reality settled in.

December marked our lowest point. Karen and Ian helped us as much as they could, but we couldn't expect them to support us. I was getting continuous news from home that people were telling the sinister tales of M.J. and how he was a thief and liar who ripped off so many good people. It was soul crushing, but I knew I had to keep it from Pete and continue looking forward. I couldn't slip back into a depression and check out again. It was not fair to him.

Money was so tight that we had weeks during which I ended up going to soup kitchens for food. There, they handed out bags with items like flour, eggs, and canned goods to whoever need it, no questions asked. I was so grateful yet so ashamed that my life had come to this.

There were some days when we had nothing but flour and salt in our cabinets, so I would mix them together in a bowl and bake the dough. We called it "Jesus Bread" and ate that for a meal. Pete was so tired of living this way, but, saint that he is, never made me feel bad about it. Of course, that only made me feel worse about myself. I didn't deserve someone this kind, loyal, and loving.

As Christmas approached, there was literally no background work to be had, and Pete realized that the only jobs he could get were up in LA. I was not a fan of LA. It was too far a commute and too crazy a place. I also was tired of the inconsistency of background work. I needed a real job that could help get us stable. We decided that after the first of the year, we would redouble our efforts pounding the pavement but turn our focus to Orange County. Until then, though, Pete and I put our troubles on hold to celebrate our first Christmas in California with Karen, Ian, their daughter Vanessa, and one of my favorite friends in the world and my old neighbor in Amsterdam, Brea, who had come to spend the holiday with us. Having Brea around made me happy whether I wanted to be or not.

It was the first time in my life that I was away from my family on Christmas, and I was pretty sad that I wasn't going to be able to see them. I also had never been in a warm climate for the holidays, and in my book, a *real* Christmas equals a *white* Christmas, or at least a really cold one. I got over all of that really quickly though, lying on the beach on Christmas Eve with people who I loved so much as we looked up at the snowflakes decorating the pier.

On Christmas Day, Karen and I split duties and cooked a big dinner for everyone to enjoy. We reserved the little room in the complex's clubhouse that had a big table, couch, and TV. We sat around, ate a ton of great food, and watched Christmas movies on TV. That night, for some strange reason we decided to cap off the night with watching the movie "*Beaches.*" Such an odd movie to watch on Christmas, but it made for a great memory. We all had a great holiday.

This really was a milestone for me. Up until then, I thought I couldn't be anywhere but home for Christmas. I mean, I actually thought that in all ways you could take it. I thought that I couldn't emotionally handle not being there, that my family wouldn't allow me to not be there, and that I wouldn't feel that the holiday happened had I not been there, but now I knew that these beliefs weren't the case at all. I had my first Christmas with my new "framily" in my new life, and although I missed my family at home, I really appreciated every minute of this time.

Four days later, however, another milestone approached. It was my birthday. My thirtieth. The night before my birthday, I laid in bed, sickened that I was turning 30 under these conditions. I thought back to this list I'd made when I was a kid of things I wanted to accomplish by the time I turned 28. I knew I was turning 30, but the list seemed more significant at this stage of my life than it did at 28. The story behind the list was almost as ridiculous as the list itself, but it was also so typically me.

When I was younger, I used to sleep over at my maternal grandmother's house all the time. It was my favorite place to be. We would stop at the store on the way to her house and buy something to make for dinner, Little Debbie Peanut Butter Bars, and Cocoa Puffs cereal. After we got home and had dinner, we would have our Little Debbie dessert at the table, then go and watch TV.

As it was usually a Friday night, we would watch our favorite show, *The Golden Girls*, on NBC. Before it started, my grandmother used to take two coffee filters and fill them with Cocoa Puffs, and that would be our snack to eat while watching the show. It was a bizarre tradition that started one night because all the bowls were in the dishwasher, and it ended up turning into "our thing".

One particular Friday, we were watching *The Golden Girls* with our coffee filters filled with Cocoa Puffs, and the episode centered around Dorothy finding a list of all the things she had hoped to accomplish by the time she turned 50. She was very distraught because she hadn't accomplished any of them, and to make matters worse, she was well past 50! In the next 30 minutes, hilarity ensued as the girls helped Dorothy feel better about where she was in her life and to appreciate all the things she did accomplish. For some strange reason, however, that episode and that idea of letting time slip through your fingers really blew my little mind.

I thought of that episode many times through the years and realized that it was a very common story line for many classic shows. This idea of time and what you make of it really was important to people. So when I was around 18 years old, I made my own list of things I wanted to do. I gave myself the cutoff age of 28. After all, that was pretty damn old, right?

Here were the items on my list:

1. Be in a boy band or on TV
2. Live in Ireland
3. Be skinny
4. Travel
5. If #1 doesn't work out, then own my own business at least
6. Figure out a way to have some type of love in my life without anyone knowing

Before I realized it, I was 27 and very much aware that it was the year to finish off my list. I have to admit, I was pretty impressed with myself. At this point, I had lived in Ireland and The Netherlands, traveled all over Europe as well as various other places in the world, had found the love of my life and didn't need to hide it anymore, and owned my own successful bar. The only thing I hadn't accomplished was the whole skinny thing, or at least, I didn't think I had. I wasn't on TV at that point and I was too old to be in a boy band now, but hey – accomplishing four out of six wasn't too bad.

Unlike Dorothy and all those other fictional characters who couldn't achieve their goals, I did, and I felt pretty good about that. Here's the problem with making life goals when you are 18, however: your goals are very short term, you don't really know what is important to you yet, and you don't know where your life is going to take you. Yes, some of my goals were important and good for my well-being, but most of them were just superficial, silly things I thought I should achieve. I never thought about what I wanted past 28 and what would be important for me in the long term.

Now, the night before my 30th birthday, I laid in my

bed and thought about all that I had and all that I had lost. Was I worse off than Dorothy? Did I actually achieve anything? I was 30, and I had done a lot in those years. I had traveled the world and seen many amazing places. This was an achievement I didn't regret and one that couldn't be taken from me. I had found a partner who truly cared about me and my well-being and who I knew I would be with until the day I died. Again, an achievement, and really, the most important achievement of my life. Unfortunately, it wasn't these things I was focusing on.

I continued to lie in bed for hours thinking about the other things I worked so hard for, achieved, but ultimately lost. I wasn't skinny. Actually, at this point, I was so obese that when I looked in the mirror, I didn't even recognize the face looking back at me. I really mean that, too. Sometimes I would stare in the mirror and try to find my face, but the one that looked back was just a stranger I refused to acknowledge. I had wasted so much time trying to be skinny and creating horrible food issues that now skinny was no longer important. My health was an issue. Who knew that at 30, I would be hoping I wouldn't have a heart attack or get diabetes. That was definitely not on my list.

As for my career, well, I had no idea what I was going to do. When the bar failed, I had lost everything and was bankrupt, so getting on my feet and starting over seemed like a huge undertaking. Never once did I think that I would be 30, unemployed, bankrupt, obese, and have so many people against me in my life. I don't think any of

Rose, Blanche, or Sophia's hijinks could have made me feel better at that moment. I thought of my grandmother and was ashamed of what I had become. She was always so proud of me, and for the first time in my life, I was glad she wasn't here to see me like this. I finally fell asleep hoping that I could just skip tomorrow or at least have some distraction so I wouldn't feel so damn ashamed.

As always, Karen knew me and was on it. We'd spent the past six months talking nonstop about everything, and she really understood the pain I was in. So for my birthday, she decided to make a party, Karen style. She made me a cupcake-cake and invited me and Pete over for a wine and bacon party. This was something we invented during the months I was waiting for Pete to arrive in California. Karen, Ian, and I would get cheap red wine and dark chocolate and make bacon. We would then blast music and drink, eat, and dance until the wee hours of the morning. It sounds crazy, but it was so much fun. This is how I was going to spend my thirtieth birthday.

In the past, I had always dreamed of having a big celebration for the big 3-0. I had hoped that it would be this monumental occasion I would remember forever and that I would always look fondly on because it was a defining moment in the great life I had made for myself. I never thought I would be eating bacon and wine, dancing in a little apartment in California with just Pete, Karen, and Ian, but honestly, it *was* one of the most special nights of my life.

When going through all the drama and trauma in

Scranton, I lost so much. I no longer had any money, there were many people I once cared about who thought I was a horrible human being, and I didn't have much hope for my future. What I did have with me on this night, though, were a few people who still believed in me, supported me no matter what, and loved me unconditionally. I grounded myself with that knowledge, and I learned to appreciate what I did have – real friends and a real, loving relationship. This was an achievement that was better than any on my list.

CHAPTER 13
"Home Improvement"
You can't blame your issues forever.

After the New Year, I really struggled to keep my focus on the here and now. I was having a very hard time sleeping, and my mind seemed to be on a never-ending loop, replaying every minute of the past year and a half of my life. Since we were unable to afford TV or Internet, books were my only escape. I would go to the library, grateful to get my hands on anything that could redirect my brain from the past.

One rainy day in January, I was walking through the library's new releases, in its main section, when I saw the picture of a beautiful man's face on the cover of a book. I recognized the face immediately, stopped dead in my tracks, and grabbed the book before anyone else did. It was the recently released memoir of Ricky Martin, *Me*. As someone who graduated high school in 1999, Ricky Martin always held a special place in my heart. I couldn't hear "Livin' La Vida Loca" without thinking of high school graduation, prom, and the following summer.

When I got home to my apartment, I began reading *Me*, not really anticipating it would be anything too interesting but hoping to find some light entertainment in the pages. I couldn't have been more wrong. I found myself captivated. Ricky lived a life that most would dream of, but he had also dealt with his own inner demons. Unlike me, there were no major failures for him to write about, but other parts of his story really spoke to me.

Ricky told the story about how he was in the boy band, Menudo, and how, in the end, it was an exhausting experience that took so much from his youth. He recalled a time when he lived in New York City after turning 18, and he brought his mother to tears by telling her he was giving up the stage because he was so burned out. Eventually, though, he returned to the stage after finding a renewed love of music and performing, saying:

> If in the deepest part of yourself you feel that you are a poet, regardless of whether you are a doctor or an accountant, you shouldn't stop writing your poetry.

He continues:

> If you don't cultivate your passion, you will always feel a void. You will always feel that something is missing.

As I read about Ricky's childhood, I already felt that we were kindred spirits because of how he described his love of singing, dancing, and putting on a show. I was an entertainer from the moment I could walk, talk, and sing. Whether it was welcome or not, I would get up and do a little song in front of people at any opportunity.

If my mom wasn't careful, she often discovered I'd wandered off in the store and was singing for people at the checkout area (my favorite selections as a five-year-old were either from *Grease* or the latest video playing nonstop on MTV. I never really got into the child-oriented *Sesame Street* genre). An entertainer is who I am at my core, and Ricky's paragraph had just reminded me how far away from that person and from my passions I was.

What an epiphany for me. How did I go from the kid who dreamt every night of being a singer, thinking about being on a stage, to being a bar owner? I was the guy who, when asked what they were going to do after graduating high school, would reply, "Be an *NSYNCer or the newest member of the gang on *Friends*!" And I meant it. I used to listen to *NSYNC and take apart all the vocals, memorize them, and then sing the songs while rotating through parts. I guess I should point out that I also knew every step to every dance routine they had as well. JC – MJ? Maybe I could replace him and no one would notice! These guys were living my dream, and I spent hours imagining me as one of them.

Owning a bar wasn't my dream. Wine was certainly not my passion. It was almost like I had suffered from amnesia, and all the memories were just starting to flood back to me. The years of singing, choir, plays, musicals, and dreaming of being on a sitcom all just stopped at some point. I had repressed that part of me, but I was remembering it now, and I wanted that passion back in my life.

I was lying on the lone piece of furniture we had in our one-bedroom apartment in Huntington Beach, a futon Karen was letting us use. I shut the book very forcefully and bolted upright on the futon. Pete was standing in our kitchen, which had a window that looked into the living area. I turned to him and said, with more confidence than I'd had about anything in a very long time, "Pete, I want to move to Los Angeles and really give this acting thing a try."

Without even a second of hesitation, Pete replied, "Okay."

Within a few weeks, Pete and I were driving around Los Angeles from Craigslist ad to Craigslist ad, desperately looking for a place. We knew that living in LA would make booking background – or, even better, actual acting jobs – much easier, plus it would open up a lot more possibilities for Pete. Finding an apartment was proving to be impossible, though. Neither of us had a steady job, I had terrible credit and judgments against me, and we really didn't have much cash on hand.

Just when I thought no one was ever going to rent to us, a woman replied to an email I sent about an apartment she was renting in West Hollywood. She seemed very nice and she told me that we were welcome to look at the place and put in an application. Pete and I drove up to check out the apartment, which she titled "The happy little yellow house" on her Craigslist ad. Have you ever had one of those moments in your life where something just felt right? Well, this was the first one of those I had experienced in a very long time.

We parked our car and started down the driveway to the back house. The door was open, so we just walked in. There was a lady with a dog standing in the living room and another in the kitchen cleaning. The lady in the kitchen introduced herself as the landlord, and she invited us to look around. Pete and I looked in the bedroom, walk-in closet, and bathroom, then went through the living room to the kitchen where she was cleaning. Off the kitchen, a door led out to a back porch that had a little yard down the side of the house for the dog to use. As soon as we walked outside to that porch, I turned to Pete and said, "I want this place. This is going to be our home."

We went back in and talked to the landlord for a while, and I pretty much laid all the cards on the table. I told her that we weren't in the best shape financially and that my credit was less than perfect. She was very kind and didn't seem to judge us in the least. She explained that we would have to fill out an application and that there would be a credit check. If our credit wasn't so great, we could still get the place, but we would be required to put up extra for the security deposit. Well, that pretty much nailed the coffin – there was no way we were going to get this apartment if it was credit driven, but I decided to put in our application anyway.

A few days later, I got a call from the landlord and was told one of the most embarrassing things in the nicest possible way when she said:

"I ran your credit, and I have to tell you that you may have the lowest credit score I have ever seen!"

After I offered some flustered verbal diarrhea to try

and cover my embarrassment, she continued, saying,

"But you are definitely our kind of people, and if you can handle extra on the deposit, we would love for you to live here."

I hung up the phone and was so overjoyed I could barely breathe. This was the place. This apartment was going to be where we really would get to start fresh. I knew that Pete would find a great job here and get his life back on track, too. I didn't know how we were going to come up with the money needed, but I knew we would. Something about it all just felt right.

My excitement must have shown, too. As I was telling my good friend, Jeff, who had also recently moved to Los Angeles, about the apartment, he must have heard the change in my voice. I told Jeff about the extra deposit when he asked what I needed to move in, and he then told me to come over and get a check. Just like that, Jeff offered to help, but what shocked me the most is that he seemed like he wanted to. Another example of the extreme highs and lows of my life. Who has friends that just offer up hundreds of dollars to help? Apparently, I did.

After feeling like I was the worst human on the planet because of what went down in Scranton, it really overwhelmed me to know I still had such loyal and generous friends in my life that continued to believe in me. These acts of kindness by my dear friends marked the start of my mental recovery and healing.

I realized that if I still had people who were this wonderful to me, I couldn't be all bad. Pete, Brea, Karen, Ian, and Jeff, among others: these people knew everything about what I had done and what was happening in my life, and they didn't judge or back away from me. They actually made it a point to be more supportive of me. That had to mean something about the person I was and the friend I was to them as well. I wasn't sure what to make of such kindness, but it made more of a difference to my well-being than I realized at the time.

I started to feel like things were finally turning around. We had the money, we had the apartment, and five days later, we moved in to our new home in West Hollywood. I felt like I was home and that a path was taking shape for me and my life. I just had to work to follow it.

CHAPTER 14
"My So-Called Life"
Don't expect change without growth.

Pete landed a job at an architecture firm in Culver City within the month, and we were actually starting to bring in enough money to cover our current bills. I signed up with a service that booked background work with many agencies in LA, and I started working more and more jobs.

With Pete back at work, he started to become his old self again, and I felt relief that I hadn't completely ruined his life. With the little stability we now had, I felt like it was time for me to start really tackling my problems and cleaning up my major mess. Although I was 3,000 miles away, my debt was all still there and needed to be settled. I needed to start trying to get as much work as possible and focus on either paying everything off or declaring bankruptcy.

I was also still dealing with people telling me about the gossip that was continuing about me back home. No matter how much comfort I found in the amazing friends I did have, it still couldn't stifle the pain I felt knowing people I once cared for were talking about me, had issues with me, or had straight up cut me out. The pain of realizing that people I cared about had cut me out of their lives was brutal. Of all the things I dealt with, this was the hardest to cope with, because it wasn't just friends, it was family too. Tough or not, I couldn't let it bring me down when there were finally good things happening.

I was enjoying being on set so much and loved getting booked to do background work. The day I was booked to play a prisoner for a new TV pilot, though, showed me I was going to have to put in some major work on myself if I hoped to do this full time. When I arrived, I was told to head to the wardrobe trailer with the rest of the background actors to get an inmate uniform. I was with a handful of guys, all in their twenties and thirties, all pretty fit. When we got to the wardrobe trailer, the wardrobe supervisor saw me and yelled, in front of everyone, "Don't tell me you are supposed to be a prisoner?" Then, while using his hands to illustrate his sides expanding, he said, "Don't they know we can't accommodate every size?"

The place fell so quiet you could hear a pin drop, and all the guys around me were suddenly very interested in what was in their backpacks or whatever they thought they saw on the floor. No one would make eye contact with me. Immediately, I started sweating and shaking from head to toe. I was absolutely mortified. I didn't know what else to do but make a joke. "My thoughts exactly!" I stated, adding, "nothing like being the one to fill the fat guy quota!"

It was so degrading I wanted to cry, run, and beat the shit out of this little man all at the same time. In the end, I was literally stuffed into an orange jumpsuit and forced to spend the day with people that wouldn't talk or look at me. "Don't let the lows be too low," I repeated. I had to figure out how to keep my life in the middle ground. I kept reminding myself to take deep breaths, and whenever I could, I went outside and looked up at the Warner Brothers water tower or the hills behind the lot and remembered that no matter what, this is where I wanted to be and that each paycheck got me closer to financial freedom.

That night, I thought a lot about what I needed to help stabilize my crazy life and help me find that emotional middle ground. I knew I had a lot going on in my mind and that I was going to need some professional help to process what had happened to me and what to make of where I was at now. I researched cheap therapy options in my area and discovered that, because I was flat broke, I was eligible for not just cheap therapy but free therapy.

I had never really thought much of therapy and wasn't sure if I bought into it, but for free, it certainly was worth a shot. I figured it couldn't be much different than me pouring my heart out to Karen on a daily basis. Now that Karen and Ian had moved to Palm Springs and we were living in LA, I wasn't able to vent as easily and, to be fair, I was getting embarrassed about always unloading my issues on her. It was time to find a professional.

Although I was nervous, I hoped that maybe I would be pleasantly surprised, like I had been months ago when I auditioned for *Dexter*. Had I said "screw it" and walked away, I would have missed out on an amazing experience. Maybe therapy would be one of those things I was so glad I did! Besides, I wanted to get my life together and be happy, and I was willing to try anything to get there.

The next week, I was scheduled to meet with a therapist named Amy. The office where she worked wasn't too far from my house, so I walked. On my way down Sunset Boulevard, I passed many of Hollywood's most well-known landmarks, like the El Pollo Loco where Brad Pitt once worked, standing outside in a chicken suit to entice people to come in for a meal (ironic they put him in a costume to get people in the door, huh?). I then crossed La Brea Avenue and looked over toward Jim Henson Studios, which was once Charlie Chaplin's studio, and I smiled at the big Kermit statue standing on one of the buildings. As I continued down the street, I passed Crossroads of the World, the tourist-trap In n' Out Burger, and then came to Hollywood High School at Highland Avenue.

On the side of the high school, there is a mural of the famous people who once roamed the halls, including Judy Garland, Cher, Carol Burnett, James Garner, John Ritter, and Laurence Fishburne, to name a few. I thought about the person I was in high school and wondered what would have happened had I actually done what I truly wanted and pursued a career in show business. I loved looking at the mural because it reminded me that I was now living in a place where anything could happen and there were endless opportunities for those who worked hard enough.

When I finally arrived at the therapist's office, I had pretty much rehearsed exactly what I was going to say to this Amy woman. I wanted help, but I didn't want a stranger to know right off the bat how crazy I was or how much I had screwed up my life. I sat in the office looking around at the other people in the room and wondered what had brought them in here. I started making up stories for each person seated around me and found myself completely lost in time when a woman appeared and called my name.

I jumped up and followed her down a hall to a little room where she waved me in and offered me a seat. After I sat down and Amy had introduced herself, I opened my mouth to start my prepared speech, and to my surprise, these words fell out instead: "Hi, I just want to tell you right now that I am probably not going to tell you the truth. Things are really bad in my life, and I am probably going to try to make it sound better than it actually is."

She sat there looking at me, expressionless, and said, "Okay, why would you want to hide the truth?" I told her it was due to the intense shame I felt for what I had done. There was an awkward pause, and then I just launched into a litany of endless babble about everything that had happened over the past two years in my life. It was truly verbal diarrhea. I jumped from one thought to another, talking about people and places that were not in context, and, in my mind, I was not being clear enough about the pain and agony I'd felt over the course of the past two years.

I figured she was going to think I was a complete lunatic after this bombardment of thoughts, but when

I finally took a breath and looked up at her, I realized her eyes were locked on me. She took no time at all with a response, and with her gaze still fixed on me, said, "I find it interesting that you just described some majorly traumatic events in your life, all with the biggest smile on your face. What's that about?"

Whoa! That was not what I was expecting to come out of her mouth. I felt so horrible and felt all the pain of the past as I told my story. I felt numb and would have never thought that there was a smile on my face. What *was* that about?

I realized at that moment that therapy was going to be tough but interesting, to say the least. She was going to ask me tough questions, really make me take a look at myself, and this wasn't going to be a quick process. Part of me didn't know if I had the energy for it and wanted to sprint out of her office and never look back. Part of me was so caught off guard that I felt like I couldn't move if I wanted to. Most of me, however, was intrigued by her statement and wanted to see where this would go. It was time for me to face my demons head on. So I sat back in my chair, took a deep breath, and thought, "Bring it on, Amy!"

CHAPTER 15
"Growing Pains"
What doesn't kill you...

Over the next few months, I met with Amy every week, and man, was it tough. Many days, I would leave so emotionally drained I couldn't even speak. I would come home and either just stare at the television and zone out or, if it had been particularly exhausting, I would go straight to bed. Pete knew enough to not even talk to me on those days. I was just too drained and too emotional to interact with the world.

The therapy I received was not like what you saw Dr. Jason Seaver doing on TV. I didn't lie on a couch and talk about all the things people did wrong to me while Amy took notes and agreed. In fact, it was the exact opposite. I sat on a chair looking directly across at Amy and talked about why I had made every decision I did in my past, good and bad.

She constantly stopped to ask me questions. She wanted me to think about what it was that caused me to act certain ways. She wanted me to notice and question why I had certain, continuing patterns? Most importantly, we talked a lot about how to move on from and let go of the trauma that I had experienced.

Examining yourself and picking apart every action you take is very intense but also very informing of who you are as a person. What I started to learn is that my actions and behaviors led me to a life consisting of repeating cycles. These cycles all revolved around me doing or being something I wasn't. I would make decisions based on how I thought others wanted me to be, not on how I actually wanted to be. Every time this happened, no matter what scenario it was, it ended in failure. Eventually, for me to see that I was living this pattern and that I needed to correct it, it took a failure so big it turned my life upside down.

But why? Why was I living like this? Obviously, this behavior started way before I opened a bar in Scranton, so Amy and I started talking a lot about how I was as a kid. I told her about how I loved to sing and what a little entertainer I was, how I loved spending time with my family, and, of course, my love for TV shows. I also talked about how I always knew I was gay, even before I knew what gay was, and how that was always on my mind.

As far back as I could remember, I knew there was something different about me and, instinctively, I knew not to talk about it. It was always present in every part of my life. When I would be watching my favorite cartoon, *Thundercats*, I knew the way I felt toward my favorite character was just a little different than how my other friends felt about theirs and that I shouldn't talk about it.

I am amazed at how clearly I can remember being three or four years old, looking around me at the kids I played with, knowing something about me was definitely different. Whatever it was, I needed to make sure no one figured it out. Even as young as four, I knew I had to start putting together a character of the person I was to be, because whatever I was, it wasn't okay.

In first grade, I would sit in the circle in the morning and actually watch the other boys to see how they sat, how they talked, and what they were playing with. It was hard for me to relate to the boys, so I was with the girls a lot, and I got along with them very easily. I watched everyone: the boys, the girls, and, most intensely, the adults. I adjusted my behavior to mimic theirs. Obviously, that is what kids do when they are growing up. They learn from watching, but I wasn't learning; I was rehearsing.

One day, when I was in second grade, the kids on the back of the bus were tormenting one young boy by calling him gay. A girl asked what "gay" meant, and one of the boys was happy to explain. Through a mix of laughter and disgust, he said, "It's the most grossest thing ever. It's when a boy likes another boy for real." This was followed by jeers and sounds of disgust by the rest of the kids on the bus.

I will never forget the words or the tone in which they were spoken. My eight-year-old heart sank with a terrible dread. In my brain, however, there was something that clicked with this idea of a boy liking another boy "for real." Could I possibly be one of those people inflicted with the "most grossest" trait in the world?

Even though I knew this was the difference I'd felt my whole life, I was only eight and had a few more years until puberty, so I hoped I had time to be proven wrong. As the good Catholic school boy I was, I prayed every night to God that he would not let me turn out gay. I didn't even fully understand it but knew if it was something that people used like a curse and to put other people down, it was obviously horrible and wrong. But time marched on, and as I hit twelve, then thirteen years old, I realized it was time for me to stop begging God to not make me gay. I was definitely gay, and I had better up my game so no one would ever find out.

My mom frequently had my aunt and her friends over to our house on weeknights to chat over some coffee. They used to sit around the kitchen table, and I used to sit on the cabinet across from them and participate in the conversations. I remember looking at them and thinking about how much I loved them all, then having a wave of numbness come over me when remembering that if they ever found out what I really was, I would lose them all.

So I spent a lot of time obsessing about ways that I could hide my gayness from the world for my whole life. There was, of course, the obvious: I could be a priest. It was an appealing possibility; I could put on a show and sing in front of an audience every week. However, I knew that when I performed, I'd much rather it be in front of a packed house on Broadway or to a sold-out crowd at some famed city arena, but it could still work.

Then there was my first made-for-TV movie, a love story titled *Never to Love Again: The M.J. Dougherty Story*. This was really imaginative and twisted but practically perfect. The TV Guide listing description goes like this:

> *Young M.J. falls instantly, head-over-heels in love with a beautiful girl who just so happens to be dying from a terminal illness. Together, they show courage and compassion to the world, as M.J. sits by her bedside daily, comforting her. Eventually, the disease prevails and she dies, leaving poor M.J. all alone on this Earth. Thereafter, he would always be known as the poor young widower who never remarried after losing his one true love. (CC, TV-MA)*

As crazy as this scenario sounds, in my mind, it would have been a blessing from God (well, for me anyway) because then I could be left alone, without any questions, but still be able to lead a normal life. Clearly, neither of these scenarios was going to happen, so in time, I abandoned the fantasies.

Spiritually, Catholic school was tough for me. It was scary thinking that I would go to hell over something I couldn't control. In addition, it really made me question whether or not God was even real. The God I believed in made me who I was, and he himself was pure love. Why would he make me this way just so I could live a lonely life and then burn in hell? This did not make sense to me and it hurt me deeply. I wanted out of Catholic school, so I begged to transfer to public school in sixth grade.

Well, Catholic school might have been tough, but nothing could have prepared me for the intense cruelty and bullying I encountered when I transferred to public school. On my first day in public school, I was a shy and very sheltered 11-year-old who sat at a round table with three other boys in an art class. As I was new, they proceeded to ask me a ton of questions. I was asked things like: "What base have you gotten to?" "Have you done it yet?" "You smoke?" I was like a deer in headlights. After I answered the first question with "I don't play baseball," I was immediately ridiculed and ferociously laughed at, and I knew it was going to be a long year.

Some of the other highlights of my years in middle school included my rapidly increasing weight, intensely red, face-covering acne, and the clever nickname "M-Gay" given to me by a boy in my class. Unfortunately, this name caught on with the kids in my grade, and it was years before I left this scarring name behind me. I can actually remember kids calling me that right in front of the teachers and looking as the teacher would just turn away. With today's hyperawareness of bullying, it is my hope any teacher who heard a kid being tortured and shamed like this would never turn away so heartlessly.

It is fascinating how kids can pinpoint your deepest insecurities and use them against you just to try to make themselves feel better. Life is stressful and confusing enough for any kid in middle school; imagine trying to manage the normal pangs of adolescence while desperately working at never being you. Sure, I know you're thinking all kids at that age are trying to fit in, but for me, as for most gay youths, I wasn't worried about having the right clothes or sitting at the cool table. I was more concerned about people discovering who I really was and then having everyone in my life turn against me and hate me, inside and outside of school.

I was such a mess at this time that I rarely socialized in school, spent all my time with family or escaping into TV land, and turned to what became my life-long frenemy—food. On top of suppressing every thought or feeling that was natural to me during this time, by associating comfort with food, I began to develop a major eating disorder that has turned out to be the most consistent thing in my life.

With middle school ending, I made the decision that I was going to make my high school years enjoyable. I decided that I would have friends and that people were going to like me. I entered my freshman year with a plan: I was going to be funny and nice to everyone, no matter how exhausting and time consuming it might be. I needed to have as many people on my side as possible in case my shameful secret ever came out.

I thought of it in statistics: if I am friends with X number of people and then somehow they found out about me, well maybe 1 to 2% of my X number of friends would still like me. Makes perfect sense, right? This was how I navigated my world. Watch everyone around you, be who you think they want you to be, and keep them entertained. That was my focus and priority in school.

It was when I shared this part of my story that Amy wanted to make some comments. Right in that little snippet of my tale, where I explained how my high school years were going to go, I had definitively illustrated how I laid the foundation for the messy cycle of the life I had made. I grew up molding myself into a person who was more concerned with doing what I thought was required to be accepted than doing what I wanted to do for me. I was a people pleaser who, at my core, needed to be accepted by everyone at all costs. I also had to make sure that no one would ever see who I really was, so I created a persona that was larger than life. She described this process in a very interesting way to me.

She said that, in a way, I created a person that was whoever I needed to be for whoever I was with at the time. I also made sure this person was fun, loud, entertaining, and larger than life. I was basically dangling a shiny object in front of the world in hopes that no one ever took their eyes off that and took a real look at me. That is, if I acted the way people wanted me to and was someone that was larger than life, putting on a show people liked, they would never think to look beyond that and see what I was secretly hiding on the inside.

This was absolutely how I lived my life. As far back as I could remember, I was putting on a show, and not just the ones where I would be singing and dancing. I worked to never let anyone see what was really behind the facade of this larger-than-life personality. The irony was that when I came out and began to tell people I was gay, this behavior didn't change, because it was all I knew how to be. It wasn't that I was a two-faced, hypocritical person; I was actually trying to be a different person to meet each individual's needs.

It made my life a constant balancing act in which I was trying to juggle stories and personality traits while always continuing to stack more layers on that forever-swaying house of cards. It is what caused me to make decisions based not on what I wanted but what I felt others expected me to do. In my mind, I would actually think through how I would act to certain people in certain situations, almost like a dress rehearsal, so when the time came, I was ready. This was not normal or healthy thinking, but it was all I knew.

Before this realization, when I was on set and some arrogant person would look me up and down and ask me about where I studied acting, I would get very uncomfortable, as I had no formal training and felt inadequate. I would get a bit flustered and say that I wasn't really an actor or that I was just starting out. After this realization, when asked the same question, I would look them square in the eye and say, "I have been a working actor for 30 years. You?"

That usually got them to shut right up!

CHAPTER 16
"Saved by the Bell"
Always work toward a goal.

As my therapy went on, Amy wanted me to focus less on what happened in my past and more about where I was at now, on the person I really was, and on what I really wanted from my life. Well, that was easier said than done. I had absolutely no idea who I was. I knew that where I was at in my life now was a big mess. And my future? Seriously? I had zero energy to focus on *that*.

One day Amy asked me to give her one adjective to describe who I really was and not something that described my created persona. I was stumped. I mean, I literally couldn't give one adjective to describe myself because I never knew if the trait I thought I possessed was really me or a trait of my created persona. Was I a nice guy? Sure, but did I actually want to be, or was I just playing that role for my current situation? Was I loyal? Yes, but was I loyal because I thought I had to be or because it came naturally to me?

I really didn't know anything about myself, and I was bitter and angry that this was the reality of my life. I didn't want to have to deal with all of this. I felt like I had been through enough, and I didn't need to start trying to formulate my personality over again from scratch. I didn't mean for me to turn out this way; I was just trying to survive. Why did this have to happen to me?

I was very overwhelmed, and I continued to analyze and try to make sense of my past. I began a cycle of dissecting everything that I had done wrong in my life on a nightly basis. Night after night, my brain would immediately fixate on my past and the pain of it all the minute my head hit the pillow. Insomnia was a way of life now. I would lie in bed thinking about every mistake I'd made, every word I wished I could take back, and of all those people who hated me or thought so poorly of me…and of those who cut me out altogether. I felt so much regret.

Week after week with Amy, I continued to go on and on about how I couldn't handle how much I had ruined my life and how I never wanted this to be my reality. I obsessed on how I really thought people knew that I cared so much and, even though it was obvious I had issues, I never thought my issues were affecting other people so dramatically. I also told her my thought that I would grow out of them or something and that everything would eventually be okay in the end for me. I certainly didn't think my life was going to be defined by my issues in the eyes of everyone I knew.

I continued to dwell on the shame, regret, and anger I felt. It seemed to me that I was getting worse. My anxiety was almost paralyzing as the weeks went on, so Amy gave me tools to try to understand what triggered the anxiety, but I halfheartedly tried to follow through on them. I was really starting to get sick of these sessions.

Had I actually been paying for them, I probably would have stopped. I thought that by this point, I would have had an improved state of mind and attitude from going each week. I did not anticipate that dissecting my issues was going to make me unable to think of anything else. It was really starting to get to me, and frankly, I was unbearable to be around. This was the last thing Pete deserved after all he had put up with. He finally felt like things were moving forward, and here I was, so moody, anxious, and overtired that I couldn't hold a conversation without biting his head off. Like always though, Pete saw the bigger picture and never made me feel bad about my actions. He just supported me as usual.

Regret is a very hard thing to deal with because there is absolutely nothing you can do to change your past. It is even harder to deal with if you can't see where you're at in life or what your future holds. I never wanted my life to be like this, but this agonizing over my mistakes did, however, help me realize one thing clearly. I genuinely cared about people, and my desire to be a kind, genuine guy with integrity was definitely who I was and who I should focus on being. How to get from here to there, though; that was the mystery.

One morning, after lying awake all night due to racing thoughts and anxiety, I actually fell asleep and had a very interesting dream.

I dreamed that I had just arrived home to Clarks Summit to attend a retirement party for my favorite teacher from high school, Mr. Campbell. Mr. C was the choir director, and I had him for four years. He was the type of teacher who actually knew his students. He knew me, my dreams, my problems, and most importantly, he was a person that I trusted completely. Even after graduation, I managed to drop him a line here and there, just to try and keep him in my life. He made that much of an impact on me.

In this dream, I arrived at his house for the party. When I walked through the living room, I saw my best friend and old Colorado roommate Nathan standing there. I was so relieved to see another face I trusted, as I was a bit anxious being back in Northeastern Pennsylvania. As Nathan was a student of Mr. C's as well, he also came in for the send-off. He walked with me toward a large staircase and told me Mr. C was upstairs, waiting to talk to me. I climbed the stairs and saw Mr. C standing in front of what looked like a balcony covered by huge red, velvet curtains, the kind you see at a theater (you know the kind I mean: like the ones that open at the beginning of *The Muppet Show*!).

I hurried over, excited to see Mr. C, but also wondering what he had heard about me and how much he knew of my failures. I was so anxious that he was going to be disappointed with me. When he saw me, he put his hand on my shoulder and smiled. He told me that he wanted me to go over to that big, red curtain, pull it back, and look down to what was behind it. He continued, urging me to really take some time and think about what I was seeing. This really confused me, but if Mr. C says do something, I do it.

I walked over and pulled the rope that retracted the curtain. It took me a few minutes to realize what I was looking at, but once I got a good look around, there was no mistaking what it was. I was looking down at the gymnasium of my high school. I could see the scoreboard on the wall that read "Abington Heights High School" and the many banners hanging around the gym commemorating the various sports championships won over the years.

In the back of the gym, sitting on the floor, was a kid wearing a red, V-neck fleece sweater and a pair of carpenter jeans. His hair was gelled and pushed up in the front. I recognized that fleece in an instant as my favorite from high school. I had bought it when the Gap first opened up in the area and it was still a big deal to have Gap clothes. My heart began racing, practically pounding out of my chest. It was pounding so hard that I could hear and feel the blood in my neck as it rushed up and down my arteries. I couldn't believe what I was seeing: I was staring down at me at 18 years old.

I stood, dumbfounded and transfixed, for what seemed like an hour before noticing steps to my left that led down to the gym floor. "Wait, can I get to him – I mean, me?" I wondered. All that was stopping me was a small velvet rope. I became both anxious and excited, and before I realized it, I was unhooking the rope and starting down the steps. When I reached the bottom of the steps, the stairs and everything behind me disappeared.

Now, standing on the floor of the gymnasium, I made my way across the floor. Never taking my eyes off of my younger self, I thought, "This is it, this is my chance! I am going to get to fix this life that I have ruined. I am going to get to spare him screwing up like I did. I can tell him about all the mistakes I made and how to avoid them. He's never going to go through the pain and feel the shame that I have!"

As I walked over, 18-year-old M.J. was now looking at me with a puzzled look on his face. My mind was racing through the timeline of my life since high school, reeling through all my past experiences, trying to figure out what I should tell him to do and to avoid. This is exactly what was going through my mind: *Okay, well first, tell him not to go to college and do...well, no, I can't tell him that because then I wouldn't have met...okay, well then, I have to tell him about that time when I... well, no, I can't tell him that either because if I didn't go there, I would not have found out about this, and that was such a good thing. Okay, well at least I have to tell him not to even move to Scranton or open the bar...but if I hadn't gone there, I wouldn't be in California. I really love it here, and if things didn't end in such a disaster, I never would have had doing background as my only work option and I wouldn't have gotten to work on a television set.*

I then thought of that mural on the side of Hollywood High School and thought of the feeling it gave me: "This is actually where I was meant to end up. My life here, right now, is what's right for me."

I realized that young M.J. had figured out who I was by now, and he was clearly shocked at my appearance. His face was as white as a ghost, and he looked like he was about to scream and run away.

I called out to him and told him to not be scared and that we were just given the most miraculous gift in the world. I was just about ready to sit down with him when it all sank in: *There isn't one thing about my past that I can have him change. Even through the worst parts of my life, something wonderful came out of it, be it a new person in my life or an experience that I either cherish or learned from. Plus, everything absolutely had to have happened the way it did for me to get to where I am right now in California. I never would have ended up here without my life progressing exactly the way it had and, for the first time in my life, I am where I know I belong. This is where my true life will actually begin, and I WILL find inner peace and happiness.*

As I hit the floor with a thud, sitting across from the younger version of me, I just started to cry. He has no idea what is coming his way. He has no way of knowing that the pain he is going to feel will be so deep and so exhausting. I wanted to hug him. I wanted to walk over, hold him, rock him, and assure him that he is a good person. Instead, I looked up at him and said this:

> "The next chapter of your life is going to be really difficult. You are going to have happy times, but they will be trumped by major tragedies and failures. The bad times will feel too overwhelming for you to get through, but there is nothing you can do to avoid them, nor do you want to. There

are going to be times that you want to
give up, and even when you think it is
time to give up, just know that you are
going to be okay. You will be okay. I
am going to be okay. It will all be
okay."

The loud school bell rang out, indicating time to
move to the next class. I woke up with the sound of
the bell ringing in my mind and already felt that
something inside me had shifted.

I felt a weight lift from me and rose that morning
calmer than I had in my whole life. This was my life.
It was my path whether I wanted it to be or not. My
path was what happened. Regret is a waste of my
energy. I can regret as much as I want, but it isn't
going to change one thing. I lived, I learned, and now
it was time to move forward.

CHAPTER 17
"Glee"
Listen to your gut.

I don't know what your opinions are or what you believe, but let me tell you this: therapy works! I'm not talking about drugs, either. I am advocating the value of sitting with a professional who knows how to help you understand your own thoughts and behaviors. Like most things in life, however, you only get out of it what you put into it. Since I'd developed such a strong desire to change how I'd been living my life, I was open to the process and, even when I thought therapy wasn't working, I didn't give up.

With the help and tools I gained from Amy, I was able to start moving my life forward in a real way that was different from how I had lived before. I made smarter decisions that improved me and my life, and I learned how to modulate my emotions when I was dealt a blow. Yes, Uncle Jerry! I was finally learning how to keep things in the middle.

Having a clearer mind gave me more energy to

focus on what I needed to do. So finally, I started making a real, concrete plan to move forward. The first thing I knew I had to do, even though I was not looking forward to the process, was to officially declare bankruptcy and lift the burden of the bill collectors, judgments, and harassment.

Although I was working and Pete had a steady income, we were barely making enough to get by. I knew that at this rate, it would be a long time before I would be making enough to pay my debts back. It was also clear by now that any money I thought I would get from Meg and our agreement was never going to be honored. Although I didn't feel ill will toward her, at this point, I realized that I had put my faith in the wrong friend and backed the wrong horse in Meg. Just another bad decision for the books. Bankruptcy was now a must.

I did some research and found a law group that specialized in bankruptcy and had the best rate. I met with them, and they informed me that my case was pretty standard and that with my signature, the filling out of some paperwork, and a check for $1,500, I could get the process started. I clearly didn't have $1,500 to give them, but we arranged a payment plan. Signing those papers that day brought me another onslaught of emotion, but luckily I was better equipped to handle it.

At first, I felt pretty ashamed about filing for bankruptcy; I never wanted to resort to it. If I hadn't been treated so terribly by certain creditors, I would have made sure I paid them every cent, even if it took me a decade. Unfortunately, I was still being harassed. Even now, living 3,000 miles away, it continued via Facebook and email and through consistent gossip spreading back in Pennsylvania. I had no choice.

I learned some interesting things about the process along the way that made me feel a bit better. I had always thought of bankruptcy as this irresponsible thing people did when they wanted the easy way out. Then I learned that Abraham Lincoln declared bankruptcy because he was struggling to pay back loans, and Walt Disney also filed for bankruptcy just a few years before creating Mickey Mouse. I discovered that bankruptcy was a constitutional right put in place so people can have a second chance when they get in over their heads. Thank you, founding fathers!

I assumed that people may have taken advantage of the process, but I knew I wasn't. My hesitation toward the process melted into gratitude. I felt very appreciative for the opportunity to have a fresh start, and it made me feel a sense of determination to work hard so I could contribute back to the system that was helping me so much.

With my bankruptcy in place, I felt that I needed to get a steady, 9-to-5 job. Although I loved being on set and was enjoying learning about and exploring the entertainment industry, I thought that it was very unfair to rely on Pete to bring in the sole steady paycheck. After all he had done for me, I wanted to start taking some pressure off of him, so I applied for a job at a bank again. I was hoping that maybe now, after some time had passed, I might be able to land a job.

I went through the first round of interviews again

and was thrilled when asked back for a second one. To me, this was an indication that my life was definitely moving in the right direction. I went to the second interview and was asked back for a third. I was pretty shocked at how intense the process was, as I was only applying for a teller position, but I was happy to continue. After that interview, I was told that I would be notified by one of the managers if I was selected to be a teller. A few days later, I received word that I had indeed been offered a job as a teller at a branch in West Hollywood, which apparently was a coveted position.

It was now December, and I was going to be starting in January. I went through the rest of December doing some more background work and ended up having a pretty good month, financially. I also had a lot of fun that month, learning a lot about the industry and meeting some great people. It really pained me to give it up, but I knew I was going to be able to work my way up from teller in no time and start making good money. Before too long, Pete and I would be pretty comfortable in our lives in California, and the nightmares of the past would be a distant memory.

Pete had the week between Christmas and New Year's off, so we spent a lot of time hanging out and talking. It was funny, but I was getting the impression that Pete might not have been too thrilled about the idea of me going to work at a bank. I talked to him about it, and he admitted that he worried that I was going to hate it and be miserable. I assured him that even if I did, I would stick it out for at least a year or until I found something better.

As January approached, I had to confirm that I would be starting training with the bank. I became more and more anxious about committing to a corporate job after doing something as exciting as working on set. I decided to tell Pete that I, too, was having mixed feelings about going to work at the bank. I told him I thought it was important for me to take this job so I could start pulling my weight and so he didn't have so much pressure on him.

In a very Pete tone, he simply said, "Well, that is ridiculous." He continued telling me that he never saw me more excited than when I was working on sets. He thought that I had finally found something that I was going to thrive in, and he really didn't mind me taking the time to explore it because he believed I would do well.

Have I mentioned how lucky I am to have Pete in my life? I find myself, more times than I can keep track of, looking at him and feeling luckier than anyone else in the world – even in hard times. I was so touched he felt this way about me and my abilities, and to be honest, I kind of felt the same way, too. I really believed that I could make something of myself in the industry. I didn't think I was going to be an Oscar winner, but I definitely could see me being "that guy" who does a bunch of commercials or day-player roles, and I would be very content with that. Besides, I wouldn't want an Oscar anyway – my sights were set on an Emmy!

After that conversation, I thought about it a bit more and realized that I lived in Hollywood. I could work at a bank anywhere in the world, but where else could I get a chance to do work like this? So I pulled up my email from the bank recruiter and emailed him, saying that I was very appreciative of the offer, but I would have to decline at this time. I went to bed feeling excited and confident about my decision.

I woke up wondering what the hell I was thinking and wishing I could magically take that email back.

I spent the first week of that New Year beside myself, amazed at my lack of common sense and my ability to make every bad decision possible. I could have just spent a year or two working at a bank, saving money, getting financially secure, and then gone back to working on sets. It didn't have to be so now or never. The entertainment industry wasn't going anywhere, after all. But the decision was made, and I had to make the best of it.

Just a few days after the New Year, I got a call to work on the show *Glee*. I was annoyed by this for many reasons, let me just tell you. First, I had barely slept the night before and never dreamed anyone would be filming right after the New Year. I was tired, I hadn't done any laundry, and I hadn't yet gotten a very-long-overdue haircut.

Second, I really did not like the show *Glee*. It got on my nerves. You would think, as a gay, musical-loving, high school choirboy, I would have loved it, but this was not the case. I think there was a part of me that was a bit bitter that it was now cool to sing and dance, whereas when I was in school, if you sang and danced, you were gay. The combination of me being cranky and my irrational bitterness toward *Glee* made me hate that I had to accept the job, but this was the path I chose, so how could I say no? I almost felt like this was the universe slapping me upside the head and saying, "This is what you get for being stupid."

I got dressed to leave for the studio and had nothing nice to wear. I ended up having to wear an old, ratty long-sleeve shirt and took some horrible old thrift-store clothes with me for a second option if needed. This was very uncharacteristic of how I usually went to set. I always made sure I arrived very early, dressed appropriately, with the best clothing options possible, and always with my best attitude. On this day, I arrived looking like I rolled out of bed and wanted to beat someone up.

When I checked in, I was directed to wardrobe, which was never my favorite place to go. I got to the trailer and went up the steps to find two very nice women busy getting things done. One woman told me that I was in for a very fun day, as it was a really small shoot with just one of the main actors, the guest star, and a few background.

Normally, I would be thrilled to make small talk and would have chit-chatted for as long as time allowed, but today I just wasn't having it. I flashed a fake smile, nodded my head, and gave a very curt "that's nice, uh-huh" response to her. It didn't seem to bother her at all. She continued on about how the guest star was one of the nicest people she had ever worked with and how he was so stunning to look at. She was really getting on my nerves at this point. Finally, she told me what to wear, and I started down the stairs of the trailer.

As I walked down the stairs of the trailer, I saw the door of the trailer across from me open. A man appeared and looked right at me, flashing a big, dazzling smile, said hello, and walked down the steps to a production assistant who was waiting to take him to set. My legs started to shake, and I had to grab the railing because they almost came out from under me. I was instantly sweating from head to toe, and my mouth was as dry as a bone. I was about to walk on set and spend the day sitting in a classroom with about four other extras, Matthew Morrison, who played Mr. Schuester, and the guest star, *Ricky Martin*.

The universe was indeed telling me something on that day, which happened to be exactly one year from the day I'd checked out the Ricky Martin book from the Huntington Beach library. During that day, Mr. Martin came over and sat on the table where I was seated. I was sweating so badly that the palms of my hands were actually wet. As a general rule, background is never allowed to talk to the talent on set, but today, I was going for it. The universe would've been annoyed had I not!

As he sat on the table, I said hello, and he turned and said hello back. He asked me my name, and we exchanged pleasantries. He had one of the kindest dispositions I have ever encountered in a human being. It really was something. Just the way he spoke and looked at you while you talked was kind. I could tell he listened and genuinely cared about whomever or whatever had his attention at that moment. They were ready to start rolling, and he got up to leave. He turned back quickly and smiled, saying that it was so nice meeting me. I couldn't wipe the smile from my face.

This single moment proved to me, more than

anything else in this world could have, that I was right where I was supposed to be, that I had made the right decision for me, and that I was going to be better than okay. In 1999, when I was graduating from high school and the radio seemed to be playing "Livin' La Vida Loca" on a loop, who would have ever thought that the man known for shaking his bon-bon would turn out to be so influential in my life? Never would I have ever thought that I would one day be making small talk with him on the set of a hit TV show, either.

Karen really knew what she was talking about on that cold, snowy night back in Scranton when she said, "the best things in life just sorta happen!" Because they just do, if you let them. To this day, I keep that copy of Ricky Martin's book on my desk, right next to my computer, where I can't miss seeing it, so I never forget how the universe and Ricky Martin helped keep me on track not once but twice.

CHAPTER 18
"The Biggest Loser"
You are your best resource.

After my new best friend and unknowing life coach Ricky Martin had convinced me that I was on the right track in my career, it was time for me to tackle the last piece of the puzzle for me. I had to figure out how to take control of my health and start making peace with that man I saw looking back at me in the mirror. This was not going to be easy, as I had a lifetime of weight struggles. I had many excuses to justify my unhealthy lifestyle, but those excuses weren't holding up anymore as other areas of my life started to improve. I would never be the man I wanted to be if I didn't get my health under control.

I had been on a diet for as long as I could remember. Most of my earliest memories revolve around my mother, my aunt Mary Eileen, and my grandmother sitting at a table, drinking coffee, smoking cigarettes and talking about how fat they were and how they needed to go on a diet. It was a weekly occurrence; every Saturday my grandmother and aunt would either come to our house or we would meet them out at a restaurant and we would have some breakfast while they had their coffees, smoked, talked about weight, and, in the spring and summer, planned out what yard sales we would hit up.

As much as I enjoyed spending the time with them, their words unfortunately began to sink into my young psyche. Here were three women, none of whom were fat, who were constantly obsessing over their weight. Before I knew it, I was five years old and telling my cousins that I couldn't eat that slice of cake because I was on a diet. I was a very cute, blond-haired, thin kid, but in my eyes, I was already fat.

I remember lying in bed at night and thinking, "Tomorrow I am going to start my diet!" This wasn't a once-in-a-while thing, this was usually right in between my daily "please God don't let me be gay" prayer and my recap of how people talked/ sat/walked/laughed today. The diet I would attempt to start was as absurd as me thinking I had to go on one. To me, a diet meant I could only eat things that were low fat or fat free, and only after trying to go as long as I physically could throughout the day without eating at all. The goal was to eat as few calories a day as possible. Achieving that meant I had a good day of eating. Nourishing my body was never a concept that crossed my mind.

I knew that sweets, snacks, fat, high-calorie foods were "bad" and fruits, vegetables, low-calorie foods were "good," but I didn't have any idea what my body needed and didn't understand that the important thing was to be nourishing myself. As I got older, my idea of a good or bad day, diet-wise, became more extreme. A good day was eating nothing except for maybe a salad with chicken for dinner, and a bad day was when I ate more than once or had anything with high calories.

When I went to college, I started my unhealthy cycle that continued for almost a decade. I would gain 10 to 20 pounds and then lose it every few months. I had the remarkable ability to gain 10 to 15 pounds in a week, but then would just starve it right off a few weeks later. Purging also started around this time and was something I struggled with for years. Even with a few extra pounds back then, I was far from fat. No matter how thin I was, when I looked at myself, all I saw was a fat guy. In reality, from the ages 17 to 27, I wore size 32 or 34 pants, and being 6' tall, that's anything but husky.

Even though I was convinced I was fat, I received a lot of attention for my looks. I was often told that I was "hot" or that I looked like some celebrity actor. I always immediately replied with something along the lines of, "You must be crazy!" and would become uncomfortable from the attention, because I assumed people were feeling sorry for me and just trying to make me feel better about myself. I couldn't see the young, fit man in the mirror – all I saw were flaws and fat.

Binge eating, purging, extreme yo-yo dieting, and a completely distorted body image added another layer of complicated issues to my already-stressed brain. Eventually, my stubbornness won out over my body, and the fat guy I always insisted I was finally came into being. This bears repeating, because it is very important to people who have body image issues; I made myself into what I feared. Like so many others, I created a self-fulfilling prophecy.

Once I became that obese man, I treated my body like a junker car that wasn't worth an oil change because you knew it would be scrapped soon. I was so disgusted with myself that I wouldn't look in a mirror and avoided photographs at all costs. I would even miss events like weddings or parties because I was too ashamed for people to see me.

The level of hatred I had for myself was so deep that I thought I had to be the first to let people know what a fat pig I was so any awkwardness could be avoided. I thought it was essential for people to understand that I was well aware of how disgusting I was. I knew that the new me I was creating for myself in California would not allow this to continue, but I simply didn't know how to fix it. Therapy had helped me discover why I had my weight issues, and now I had to learn how to change them.

It is easy to say, "just go on a diet and exercise," but when someone has weight issues, there is much more to it than just that. People don't overeat because they are always hungry; most of the time, it is in response to something happening in their life. Food can become a drug of choice that can lead to severe addiction. I feel that eating disorders should be treated like any other type of addiction due to the fact that the user becomes a slave to finding his or her next fix. It is proven that food can trigger chemical responses in your brain that make you feel certain ways, thus compelling you to repeat the behavior that led to the response in the first place. Research has also shown that sugar lights up the very same part of the brain that's triggered by cocaine or heroin.

This made a lot of sense to me, because I knew I was addicted to food. Back in Scranton, when I wouldn't get off the couch to go to work, visit friends, or even get the mail for fear of running into someone, I would still plot out a route to go to the store or a drive thru to get my next fix. The need for the food trumped my fear of seeing people, and the process of getting it, combined with the ritual of how I would consume it, was itself a high.

One of the hardest parts about having a food addiction is that you can never stop having food. If you are addicted to alcohol, cigarettes, or gambling, for example, after you get through treatment, you can simply avoid being around it. It is different with food; you will always have to eat. There is no escape from it. I knew that it was one of the last obstacles, and maybe the biggest, in becoming the new me I was working toward, but I wasn't sure how to retrain my brain in this category. I had made a big step in therapy in learning the why behind my issues, but now I had to figure out the how.

I decided I was going to join a gym, but that ended after a whopping single visit. Starting at a gym when you are significantly overweight is hard enough, but it is even harder when you don't really know how to use weights or the equipment. Now add to the mix the fact that I was in Hollywood, where everyone looks like a model, and I was literally running out after a few minutes.

When it came to diet, I struggled a lot because I was always trying to eat the lowest amount of calories possible, so I could lose the highest amount of weight the fastest. The problem there was that I would get really far into the day, then completely snap and eat everything in sight. After I snapped, I would feel so bad about failing that I would make plans to start again tomorrow and continue eating whatever I wanted for the rest of the day for my "last meal."

I couldn't break this cycle and didn't have the money to seek professional help via a trainer or nutritionist. I was becoming very frustrated, and a hint of defeat started entering my brain. However, I was trying not to let this low get too low and lose sight of the good in my life, so I kept looking for a solution.

I came across an ad for a documentary looking for participants willing to commit to a program in which they would learn how to eat right, exercise, and lose weight. The advertisement said that meals would be provided, as would a trainer, and participants would be compensated for their time, as well as be required to live in a house for a few months in the Hollywood hills. It sounded either too good to be true or a little like a reality show to me, but I figured it couldn't hurt to check it out, so I applied.

I was asked to meet for an interview, and it was a very weird experience. I sat in a dance studio in Hollywood as the project's director positioned me in a chair and got me all mic'd up and ready to talk on camera. Over the course of an hour or so, this man who I'd just met asked me very personal questions about my life and the driving reasons behind me becoming overweight.

"Why do you think you are obese?" he asked.

"Nice to meet you too!" I thought.

I answered his questions with blunt honesty and was very unsure how I sounded when I thanked him for the opportunity as I left. I heard back from him a few days later, and he let me know that he was considering me for the project and that he would let me know as soon as he decided. After months of waiting, I heard the news that the director cast me in the documentary (with three other people) in which I was challenged to learn about and deal with obesity.

I was excited to learn that I had been picked to participate, but I was also worried about going through such a personal and unflattering process on film. Pete, of course, just wanted to support me with what I decided to do. He wanted me happy and healthy but didn't offer his opinion much to me on this topic. He wanted to make sure I made the right decision for me. I decided to call Karen and get her thoughts on what I should do since I knew she would have no problem telling me her opinion. As I talked to her, I knew I wanted to do it, but I felt a bit apprehensive. With a firm "Don't be stupid!" Karen put any worries I had to rest, and I mentally got myself ready to join the project.

The day I moved into the house was very exciting. I honestly didn't know what to expect but was ready to deal with whatever came my way. It reminded me of how I felt when I was tapped on the shoulder while waiting to start my first day of background on *Dexter*. Or when Amy asked me why I was smiling telling her about the traumas of my past. If there was anything I learned from those experiences, it was that if you let yourself take some risks (and manage not to freak out), the results could be very rewarding. This is how I was going to think about this new experience. Take a risk, keep composure, and have faith it will turn out.

I met my three housemates, our trainer, the nutritionist, and the doctor who would be overseeing our progress, and I really liked everyone. We were all getting to know each other and talking about how we were feeling about this whole project. Then we individually went to talk to the trainer and the nutritionist so they could get an idea of who we were and what we needed from them.

When it was time for me to meet the nutritionist, Heather, I instantly knew I'd met a lifelong friend. She was passionate about health and nutrition and was excited to share her knowledge with us. She and I chatted for quite some time, sharing stories, laughing, but, most importantly to me, being real about why we were both here. From her, right from the first week, I learned some of the most valuable health lessons of my life.

The first day we were there, she was making us some lunch and she made a chicken salad. She used grilled chicken thighs, mayonnaise (regular, not fat free!) and put it on greens with some walnuts. I watched her the whole time she was preparing and felt very suspicious. As much as I loved her already as a person, I wanted to see her credentials. Dark-meat chicken and mayonnaise? I thought we were on a diet!

Of course, I dove right in with a series of questions, doubting the effectiveness of this diet plan, but she just continued smiling and pointed out a few things to me. She told me that the dark meat has more nutrients than breasts, and the mayonnaise she was using was made with all real ingredients. She explained that it was about getting nourishment for our bodies, not about starving us. "Restriction doesn't work!" she added.

I did not understand this thinking at all. Of course a diet means restriction; mayonnaise is fattening, fat equals weight gain, case closed. I expressed this concern to her and said that it made no sense to me. I continued to tell her that the one thing I did know was that to lose weight, I needed to make sure I kept my calories as low as possible. After all, in my day, I had done every diet program out there.

With a smile on her face and in the sweetest way possible, she turned to me and said, "Oh yeah? How's that been working out for ya?" Ouch! Touché. I decided to keep my mouth shut from that point on and embrace the whole process. Heather was right; nothing I had been doing was working out for me, so I needed to relinquish control.

That first week, I lost 11 pounds. By the end of the first month, I was down 30 pounds and lost 6 inches on my waist alone. I lost all this from daily activity and from eating, and eating a lot. I felt like every time I turned around, Heather had another meal or snack for us to eat. What the premise of the documentary came to be was this: when you are obese, your body is actually malnourished. Pre-packaged, processed, fast foods and the like don't provide your body with the nourishment, vitamins, or minerals it needs to work properly. So, as your body continues to be deprived of what it needs, it thinks it is starving and starts packing on the pounds with whatever it is given to ensure survival. What I learned, and what really worked for me, is that the best way to beat obesity is to feed it.

I fed my body whole foods and greens and kept away from all packaged and processed foods. Within six months, I had lost 100 pounds and was back to wearing the clothes I had in my early twenties. More importantly, my thinking started to change when it came to my relationship with food. I realized food was more than what made you gain or lose weight, and it was not going to cheer me up or make my problems go away, either.

I learned, and more importantly started to feel, that food was energy. When I switched to this diet, I had real, sustained energy from morning to night for the first time in my life. I used to wonder how some people I knew could get so much accomplished during the day and never seemed to be tired. I thought they were just lucky. I didn't realize that anyone could have it if they only gave their bodies the proper tools. Once I started having energy, I was hooked! Having energy in your day makes life a whole lot easier to handle, and it feels much better than any high I received from eating junk food.

As soon as I lost my weight and the documentary drew to a close, I started getting a lot more work as well. Going to the wardrobe line was no longer a cause for major anxiety, either. I just would go and get what I needed without a big production. I felt such a sense of accomplishment and relief that I'd finally conquered this beast, and I started to think that my life of drama and trauma was fully behind me now. I'd put so much work into myself, and I was finally seeing and feeling the results of that hard work. It felt good.

CHAPTER 19
"Grey's Anatomy"
Cherish meaningful moments.

I was struggling to see and gain focus of the room around me. I was so cold and all too aware of the plethora of people buzzing about. I was wrapped pretty much from the waist up in gauze and tape. My face, shoulder, and neck, in particular, were heavy with the weight of materials and equipment. I could feel liquid caked onto my skin and puddled under my back. Tubes were taped to my hands, and I realized if I moved, I was probably going to do some kind of damage, so I just laid there for what seemed like hours. My nose never needed to be scratched so badly.

Time stood still, as I could only make out shadows of figures as they walked around me. The gauze was also all over my face, and I just had a small open area around my eyes to see through. The lights seemed annoyingly bright, and I was very aware how strange I must look, lying on this gurney, in this hall-lobby area of the hospital. Although it made me feel a bit uncomfortable, I didn't seem to be in anyone's way, and no one else seemed to be bothered with my presence.

I started to hear my name mentioned more and more and realized whatever they were going to be doing with me was getting closer to happening. I couldn't make out everything that was being said because I had gauze covering my ears as well. Oh, how I would have loved to have my ear scratched. Then people started popping up over me and asking if I was doing okay. I would nod my head ever so slightly so as to not mess up my mummified form. The time had finally come. The woman who seemed to be running the show came up to me and explained what was about to happen and what they needed me to do. She was very nice and sympathetic to my current state. She explained that as long as everything went smoothly, I would be done pretty quickly and would be able to get much more comfortable. That was good news.

Then it started. There were so many people around me. Everyone would pop their heads over me and introduce themselves and say who they were and what they would be doing. All I could really do was nod. I felt a little nervous and a little ridiculous. I had assumed the process was going to take a long time and that I was going to be very uncomfortable. Fortunately, they assured me that wouldn't be the case. I was being rolled around with what seemed like a team of people surrounding me. There were lots of odd noises and people throwing out a litany of medical and technical terms. I still felt awkward, but

I knew this was a good thing to be happening, and it would be over before I knew it.

There were nurses, doctors, and paramedics around me as they talked about my history and what caused me to end up in their care today. Everyone seemed confident, and it all seemed very orderly. Then, a twist – I felt a rush of liquid flowing from my neck down to the small of my back. Then pressure as someone pressed their hands against my neck.

There was an immediate flurry of action by the doctors, and my head started thrusting up and down on the gurney. The tube in my mouth made me gag, and the liquid pooling under me was nauseating. Quick chatter, hands all over me, lights shining on me. Then, it was over. All this time waiting and all of these people surrounding me did all of this for what seemed like seconds. I didn't even want to breathe, as I was so worried I would ruin something, but I didn't need to worry. It was all done, and I was finished.

The director yelled "Cut!" and announced I was "wrapped" on the set of *Grey's Anatomy*. Everyone on set clapped for me (apparently that is what they do when someone has completely finished their part on a set) and I was both embarrassed and honored. The first assistant director Annette and the producer Linda helped me get up and made me feel as if I was just as important a character as the leading stars. I saw how they made this set a place that people could enjoy their work. I was thrilled to sit up and to start getting some of this tape and gauze off of me. However uncomfortable it was, though, I felt more bummed than anything. My time on the set was over.

What an amazing, educational, and weird experience it was. I spent the last few days getting ready to be in a scene where I accidentally put a chainsaw through my nose and chest all for less than a minute of airtime. So many people and so much money were involved in making me a prosthetic nose and wound, doing my makeup, dressing my wounds, and rigging a fake blood explosion from my neck so it would all be completely accurate and believable for those who watch.

I had to lie on set all day with my shirt off, and I was very aware that the timing was perfect. Had this opportunity been a few months earlier, there would have been no way in hell I would have taken my shirt off in front of McDreamy, otherwise known as the actor Patrick Dempsey. Even though I had lost a lot of weight, having my shirt off on a Hollywood set was still cause for anxiety, but I didn't let it get the better of me.

As I said thank you to the fascinating people I'd met and made my way out, winding through the various sets of this show that I loved, I still felt overwhelmed that I was actually here. Even a year ago, if you had told me I would be working on *Grey's Anatomy*, I would have laughed in your face. I was also very aware that this experience wouldn't have happened at all had I not gone through all the rough times in my past that I was just moving on from. Without those failures, I would have never been standing here. The internal work I'd been doing toward becoming the person I wanted to be and living the life I wanted to have was finally bearing fruit.

As I got onto the golf cart that was taking me through the studio lot to the trailer where I could get changed, I just thought it was significant that this show, of all shows, was the place I first felt like I had really changed. I'd watched this show for years, and it was one of my favorites. It was a show that helped serve as an escape for me back in Scranton, and I would watch episodes back to back in order to block out the reality of my life. Now, this show was my job.

If you know me, you know that I am always singing and at all times, I have a song stuck in my head. It wasn't a surprise to anyone that for the past two weeks, I had been humming, whistling, and singing the show's theme song over and over again. As I walked up to the trailer door to change and go home, I was thinking about the words in the theme song of the show, and the irony was not lost on me. The song states this simple but powerful truth: "Nobody knows where they might end up, nobody knows!"

After my *Grey's Anatomy* experience, I took a long look at how far I had come since moving to California. I have always said that California brought me back to life, and it was very clear that this statement was true, even then. My bankruptcy had gone through, and I had worked hard in therapy. I didn't have to worry about bill collectors calling me or shaming me anymore.

More importantly, I didn't worry about what people were thinking or saying about me back in Scranton, because I realized that although I'd made mistakes, I was just doing the best I could with the tools I had at the time. I also understood that we all are doing the best we can everyday with our own individual issues.

People could throw stones, but it is less about me and more about them. It was empowering to know that I was growing as a person and that I would never fall back into the patterns of my past self.

Over the next few months, I was taking any jobs on sets that I could get, and I also got a part-time job at a gym to help keep me around healthy, active people. During this time, I was booked to do background one day for a movie starring Kristen Wiig, James Marsden, and Wes Bentley, among others. I was pretty excited because I loved Wes Bentley, I thought Kristen Wiig was the funniest woman ever, and James Marsden had been one of my favorite actors all the way back to his days as Jack Bartlett from *Sugar & Spice*.

A lot of my friends who are aspiring or working actors often look down on me for consistently taking background jobs, but I always look at these jobs as paid education. For me, I used the time to watch everything happening on the production. I found it very helpful, as I learned not only what the actor's process was but what everyone from the director to the production assistants does. In my past life, I would have been so concerned that they thought less of me for doing background, but the new me didn't care. I continued to book whatever job I could get, and this day, on this production, proved to be one of those times I was so happy I did.

The summer in LA can be a very slow time for production, so people tend to be scrambling for work. Which happened to be the case during the Wiig/Marsden/Bentley movie's filming. I arrived on set for work with the understanding that I might be called back in a day or two. While I was sitting there waiting to start, I was my normal, polite self, who watched everything and followed every direction. I happened to be standing next to Kristen Wiig's stand-in, a pretty young woman named Tanya, and we started chatting. She was very nice told me how she had been lucky because Kristen tended to take her to various productions that she had going on, thus ensuring her consistent employment.

A stand-in is one of those things in Hollywood that is pretty essential to a production but to the outside world is pretty ridiculous. Basically, a stand-in is someone who is of a similar build to the actor working a scene. The crew will match the stand-in with wardrobe of the same color as the actor then place the stand-in on the set and mark out the staging. They will set the shots for the cameras and make sure all the lighting is right and that the scene will flow smoothly. This way, when everything is set, the actors just have to come out, look for their marks, and do their scene.

It is actually a lot of work, but it is also a lot of fun. I always wanted to do it because you usually get to talk to the actors a lot, and you really get to learn about making a movie or television show in a hands-on way. The problem with getting to be a stand-in is this: you have to have stand-in experience to be a stand-in. Well, that certainly can make it difficult to break into. Plus, as a guy of significant size, I wasn't able to pass for most actors on set. I figured being a stand-in wasn't going to be one of those specialties I could add to my resume.

That day, however, the second assistant director came over and was giving notes to Kristen's stand-in. He turned to me and asked what I was doing. I said I was background. He informed me that they needed a stand-in for James Marsden and asked if I had experience. My first thought was, "Oh my god, he thinks I have a similar build to James Marsden?" That made me very happy.

As my thoughts were rejoicing that I could pass for the guy who played Cyclops in *X-Men*, my mouth responded to the question with a very confident "Yes!" He was satisfied with this answer, asked no further questions, and told me to go to wardrobe to get color matched and come back to set with the sides. (Sides are what they call the part of the script they are shooting that day.)

I had absolutely no idea what I was supposed to do and knew that every person on the crew would be working around me, asking me to do things, and I couldn't ask them to explain. I looked over at the other stand-in and just blurted out that I had never been a stand-in and had no idea what I was doing. She laughed and said not to worry. She told me to go to wardrobe and come back, so I did what I was told. For the rest of the day she directed me on what to do when I wasn't really sure of what to do. She was so nice about it, and in the end, it was very easy to follow. I got to work for almost the whole rest of the movie standing in for James Marsden or Wes Bentley, and it was such an amazing experience.

Again, just like when I was auditioning on *Dexter*, sending the email to the bank turning down the job, or in the therapist's office, I could have stepped back and kept my mouth shut, but didn't and was rewarded. By now, I was being continually reminded that taking risks was something the new me should always be doing. It is only through taking risks that anyone can hope to reach their goals and fulfill their dreams. I was starting to have dreams again so I made a mental note to take and appreciate any risks that came my way.

CHAPTER 20
"Medium"
Embrace life's curve balls.

A few weeks before I finished my stand-in work, I injured my knee in an awkward accident while working my part-time job at the gym. At first, I was very achy and stiff but thought I would be okay and it would just get better over time. After about a week, the knee was still not getting any better.

While on set standing in, there was a scene in which I had to be on my knees motioning for a dog to run over to me. After the shot was set up and everyone was moving so the actors could come in, there I was, still on the floor, unable to get up. The main actor was actually the one who helped get me off the floor, and I really started to worry about my injury now. I didn't want anything to affect my ability to perform at my job.

By the time I was done with the production, it was clear that my knee was not healing by itself, and I wasn't going to be able to be on set for quite some time. I knew that if I couldn't bring my "A game" every time I worked, then I couldn't work on set at all.

My knee injury had happened while working, so I had to enter the maddening world of worker's compensation to get it fixed. I had hoped that I could get my injury taken care of quickly so that it would be nothing more than a minor bump in the road. When I finally got it looked at, I had medial and lateral meniscus tears on my right knee and would need to have surgery. I was ready for the surgery and wanted it as soon as possible. The waiting game officially began.

Just around that time, I got some other news that caused my world to stop in its tracks. Karen had been diagnosed with cancer while I was doing the documentary, but after a few surgeries and the most ridiculous determination I had ever seen, we thought she had beat it 100%. In fact, just a few months back, I had spent a few weeks in Palm Springs doing some work, and while I was there, we celebrated how she'd conquered cancer. The past few weeks, though, she really hadn't been feeling very well and was vomiting a lot. She couldn't keep anything down, which was very worrisome. Finally, Ian took her to the hospital, and I got a call from Karen.

I answered the phone with my normal, chipper "Heyyyyyy! How are you feeling?" In response, all I heard were a few sniffles and quiet. My heart sank. I am pretty sure she was alone in the hospital room when she called me, because I couldn't hear a sound in the background. I knew it was bad. I asked, "Are you ok?"

This time, she just started crying. "They put me on hospice," was all she could get out.

I started crying as well. I don't think we said anything else. She had to go and said she would talk to me later.

I called Pete, and we made plans to go to Palm Springs that weekend to see her. Just a few months earlier, Karen had looked better than I had seen her look in years. Now she looked like a dying woman. I walked into the house and made sure I acted as normal as possible, but I had to pretend that I was in dire need of the bathroom so I could escape her eyes and cry behind closed doors.

I could see the stress and anguish in Ian's face, too. He looked exhausted and defeated. It was hard to have an actual visit with Karen because she was just too sick, but we tried the best we could. I tried to be funny and tell all the tales that had been going on in my world. Karen barely responded.

We wanted to take her to her favorite Mexican restaurant for dinner, but she didn't even make it long enough for the food to be served. I told Ian and everyone else to stay and eat. I would take her home, and I hoped Ian could get at least a few minutes' break. In the car, Karen, for the first time, really started to open up. "I am going to die," she said to me. At that point, I also knew that was the case. There was no way around it and nothing more to say, so I just grabbed her hand. As we drove, the song "Return to Pooh Corner" by Kenny Loggins played, and instead of talking any more, we just sang.

After that weekend, Karen didn't get any better, and as I was trying to keep myself busy while waiting for my own surgery, I got a text from Ian saying that Karen was back in the hospital. I didn't ask if she was okay or what was wrong, I just asked if I should come. He replied, "Yes." The next morning, I packed a few things in a bag and headed to Palm Springs. I wouldn't be home for six weeks.

When I got to the hospital and saw Karen, it was clear that she was in the end stages. She was still mentally alert and knew what was going on, but she barely resembled that vivacious young woman who mesmerized everyone she met. I took it upon myself to make sure Ian got some relief from his round-the-clock duties by staying with Karen in the hospital during the nights. This was a decision that I am still glad I made.

Every night for more than a week, after all the visitors came and left, it would just be me and Karen. She rarely slept through the night, and as the days went on, the nights became harder on her. To combat these tough nights, we talked about everything. She shared her thoughts on her dying, how she felt so sad to leave Ian and her daughter, Vanessa. She talked about things she did in her life that she really loved and things she did that she really wished she hadn't. We reminisced about good times in Scranton, fun in Huntington Beach, the Christmas we watched *Beaches* together – the irony of that was not lost on either of us. When she was in too much pain to talk, I would default to the thing that originally brought us together: music.

I would play various tunes from the sixties, seventies, and eighties. One night in particular when she was really in bad shape, I played the soundtrack from *Xanadu*, one of her favorite movies. Through the pain and what must have been a very thick mental fog from some intense drugs, Karen would continuously pop her hands up at certain parts in songs to do the dance routines as seen in the movie. These may not seem like the type of memories that make one warm and fuzzy, but if you knew Karen and knew how strong and passionate she was, moments like this made me so proud to have called her my "framily."

I would sit on the chair across from the hospital bed sometimes, just in utter disbelief that this was happening. Karen wasn't the first person I'd watched wither away and die from cancer, but she was the first close friend I'd watched decline. While I sat staring at her, my own selfishness began to kick in at times. I couldn't help but think that this had to be some kind of cosmic joke.

Here I sat looking at this woman, this friend who was now my family, the person I shared every Thanksgiving with, the person who literally put me into my career and who convinced me to do the weight-loss documentary, and she was dying. I would think how, of all the people in my life, no one, besides Pete, had been as supportive, unwavering, and encouraging as she had when I was at my lowest. It was at her kitchen table, just a few months earlier, that we'd sat making plans for my life.

She saw me as an actor, as an author, and as a motivator. I was writing this book because of her encouragement. She knew every detail of every mistake and failure I have ever made, and she saw nothing but potential, goodness, and talent in me. A major life lesson just dawned on me: losing a bar, having people think things about me, and declaring bankruptcy is not important. All those things happen, and you can learn to move on and cope. Not having your health and losing someone so essential to your life: now *that* is a hard pill to swallow.

Karen was released from the hospital to her mother's house on hospice so she could spend whatever time she had left in the comfort of friends and family. In true Karen style, she hung on with every fiber of her being until her body was reduced to nothing more than skin and bone. We were all there with her when she died, and her passing is something I will never forget. It was a very intense and emotional time that shook me to my core. No amount of work that I had done to myself could have prepared me for it.

After Karen died and I returned to Los Angeles, I finally had my surgery. By this time, it had taken so long to have the surgery that I had injured my other knee as well, and I was having a very hard time moving at all. After my surgery, I learned that the surgeon had seen that my ACL had an almost complete tear, but as it was not authorized for repair, he couldn't do anything about it.

As I started my physical therapy for my right knee, I realized I was going to have to eventually have two more surgeries, and that news was another blow to my psyche. My immobility and inability to work, combined with the daily pain I felt with the absence of Karen, did something to me I didn't think would ever happen again: I started to repeat old patterns.

I started gaining weight again, and I didn't want to go outside. I watched a lot of television and started drinking heavily. I was so frustrated that I had put so much work into myself, and it all seemed to be unraveling, that I wanted to just throw my hands up in the air and quit. I also still didn't know how to deal with the loss of Karen. I would constantly go to pick up my phone to send her a text, or I would see some article of clothing and think how I should take a picture of it to show her. The confidence I had obtained just a few months ago about how happy I would be with my future seemed to be fading from my mind more and more each day. Life really wasn't fair.

Whether I felt life was fair or not, the world kept on turning, and I found myself needing to travel back to Pennsylvania to attend two weddings. Normally, under these circumstances, I would have declined my invitations, but the two people getting married were people I would always support because they had been such supporters of me.

The first wedding was for Shana, the manager of my former bar. Obviously, she'd had to endure a lot of drama working for me. Never in the whole time she worked for me, or after, did she ever make me feel bad about anything that happened. In fact, even as I wrote this book, I talked to her to make sure all the events I was writing about were accurate, and she still was supportive of and compassionate about what I had gone through. So, no matter how depressed and fat I felt, I owed it to her to be there to cheer her on as she got married.

The second person who was getting married was my friend Courtney from college. Courtney was the first friend I had who showed me what it meant to be a real, loyal friend. When I was in college and I was still in the closet, I lied through my teeth about everything to cover up the fact that I was gay. Well, I was extremely close to Courtney, and she's no dummy.

One day, I walked into the apartment and into her room. She closed the door behind me and said, "So, are you going to quit being shady and just tell me what is going on?"

I burst into hysterical tears, and so did she. We sat on her bed and talked for what seemed like hours, and that was the first time I told someone I was gay. Without her, I don't know when I would have felt confident enough to come out, and I probably would have continued spinning the web of lies that would inevitably come back to bite me in the ass. Again, there was no excuse that could keep me from being there for her.

Going back to Scranton is never fun for me. I always feel a little anxious, but this time, I felt more anxious than I had in a while. I didn't want to be there, but since I had to be in Pennsylvania anyway, I might as well take the opportunity to see my friends and family. While I was there, my cousin Jennifer had told me that she had gone to see a medium she heard about while shopping at a local store. In the five years since my Uncle Michael died, Jennifer had not been able to move on much. She thought that maybe if this person was legit, she could get some closure. So she made an appointment and went.

Jennifer was raving about how accurate this lady was in describing not only things surrounding her father and his death, but of other people in her life that had passed, too. I was always extremely skeptical about this type of stuff, but I thought it might be kind of interesting to go and see what this woman would have to say to me. I got the information from Jennifer and I went to have a reading from this lady, along with my lifelong friend Renee, who had recently lost her husband. I really didn't care one way or another about it. I was going with an open mind but not expecting much more than some parlor tricks and an interesting conversation with my friend after.

For the record, I would like to state that this medium, Hattie, had no information about me or my friend other than the fact that I was referred to her by Jennifer and I would meet her at a specific time. The appointment was scheduled via text message on a friend's phone, so she couldn't even look up my name or number.

Before I walked into the reading, I became apprehensive and felt a bit nervous about something that had happened when Karen died. I turned to Renee and told her a quick story.

I told her about how Karen and I used to always talk about religion and spirituality. Neither of us really knew what we believed in, but we both knew we believed in something larger than ourselves. Because of my Catholic school days and being gay, I found it hard to believe in something that hated me from the start.

On the day Karen died, everyone was going into the bedroom to say their goodbyes to her. I was really not wanting to do this and held out to the last possible moment I could. When I finally went in and had some private time with her, she had been sleeping for days, completely unresponsive. I believed that her body was just going through the motions of shutting down and assumed that she was pretty much gone.

After I told her how important she was to me and how much I loved her, I leaned over and whispered this into her ear: "If you are still you when you are gone, and there is something more, I know you of all people can figure out a way to tell me about it. Please try, 'cause I am scared."

I didn't tell anyone I said this to her, because although I didn't really believe she could hear me, I worried it may have been inappropriate. I honestly didn't even believe in this medium, but for some reason I was nervous and felt I needed to tell my friend this story before we went in.

I let Renee go first and took a seat away from where they were talking. As I waited, out of the corner of my eye, all I could see was tears flowing down her face. She just kept nodding and saying "yes" to Hattie, and she was very flushed. After she was done, Renee walked toward me with a look of complete amazement, and I asked how it was. She just shook her head and mouthed, "Oh my God!" to me. It was my turn, so I walked over and sat down.

Hattie began by explaining her process and then went straight at it. She immediately started rattling off members of my family, calling some by name, telling me things about them that were completely accurate. She told me that they were showing her a book, and then she asked me if I was writing a book. I said yes. She said they were very happy about this.

She continued with other things they were sharing. Mostly it was my two grandmothers and my Uncle Michael talking, she said. They showed her I was in California, that I was acting, they showed me singing, and that they wanted me to be on a stage. This was exactly what they would be talking about. I was impressed but not convinced.

Then she said a beautiful, blonde-haired young woman, who she believed was named Karen, was with me. She said that she had cancer for two years, that we had become friends through music, that I was close to her daughter, which made her very happy, and that her husband was a piano player. All these things were true.

She continued telling me a lot of things that solidified that this was indeed Karen until she stopped very abruptly, looked me straight in the eye, and said, "Did you used to talk with Karen about life after death?"

My heart sank. I didn't say anything. She continued:

"I am getting a very strong message from her that I am supposed to say to you directly – that this is coming directly from her to you – that 'Yes! There is life after death, everything is going to be okay, and you don't have to be scared.'"

After asking if that made sense to me, I shook my head to acknowledge, yes. Before she finished my session with her, Hattie added: "Don't worry! You guys will be dancing on top of a bar again."

I was the one with tears rolling down my cheeks now. Karen was with me – she never left – and she was still encouraging me. Life might not be fair, but it certainly is amazing sometimes.

CHAPTER 21
"20/20"
You are a work in progress.

After I got home from that Pennsylvania trip, I started thinking about how there are always going to be rough patches in life. I think that after going through all the stuff that I had in Scranton with the bar, I was so focused on getting myself together that I forgot to expect more bumps along the road. Karen's death was definitely more of a sinkhole than a bump, but I knew it would be an insult to her, and to the encouragement she gave me, to let myself slide any more. Also, at this point, hadn't Uncle Jerry's advice really sunk in? I couldn't let myself be ruled by extreme emotions, because it wasn't doing anything positive either for my life or for those I loved.

Looking back over the years since I moved to California, I see that no matter what is happening in my life, fundamentally, I have changed. I guess I didn't see the real change until I started to slide backward in my life. Look at how I allowed myself to check out of life when my Uncle Michael died. Although I grieved and am still grieving Karen, I was able to pull back on the reins much quicker than before.

The changes that occurred in me that really made the difference in my life were not anything to do with my bankruptcy or how much I weighed. It had to do with how I interacted with the outside world and how I let the outside world affect me internally. I can go to all the therapy I want, eat super clean, work out every day, and pay every bill on time, but if something is going to happen that is going to affect me, then it is going to happen, and the one shouldn't affect the other. There isn't a correlation between the two things. I needed to learn how to do things for me and how to separate my emotions from my environment.

I started thinking about people in my life who I considered to be highly functioning people and wondered how they did it. I mean, they were people who dealt with issues, death, and so forth as well. How did they manage to keep their lives on track through the rough times while still being able to face whatever challenges were in front of them?

I found it funny that for someone who was a chronic mess, I had a significant amount of amazingly high-functioning people in my life, all doing really excellent things. So I devised a plan that would help me get the answers I was looking for without having to ask a bunch of intrusive questions or telling them my whole reason behind the question. I started asking these people questions regarding their daily routines and then the simple question,

"What do you think is the most important thing for you to do with your life?" I found that in one form or another, everyone had the same answer. The answer, to be perfectly honest, blew me away at first.

They all stated that the most important thing for them to do in their life was to be good to themselves. Being good to themselves was the most important thing in their life? Was that a joke? I was brought up from the school of thought that the worst thing in the world that you could be was selfish, and to me, this was being selfish. Always do for others before you do for yourself was pretty much the motto of life that was drummed into my head. I admired how these people performed in their lives, but clearly, this was not an example to follow.

But then I started thinking about these people, and I realized that they are anything but what we as a society consider selfish. So I re-examined this theory: be good to yourself. What did that mean exactly?

For one, being good to yourself meant that you had to take care of yourself above all else. That meant that if someone needed help or you were expected to do something, but it wouldn't be good for you in the long run, be it physically, mentally, or emotionally, you simply shouldn't do it. You didn't owe anyone anything that was more important than what you owed yourself. To me this was absurd, ridiculous, and just plain wrong.

After dwelling on this concept, I started wondering why it is so absurd, ridiculous, and just plain wrong. I mean, you only have one life and one body, right? Isn't it kind of your sole responsibility to take the best care of them possible? Furthermore, no matter what your beliefs are, isn't the gift of your body and your life the most precious gift we are given? Without it, we can do nothing else for ourselves, for anyone else, or for the world around us.

Maybe being selfish isn't such a horrible thing? Maybe being selfish is a necessary thing. Perhaps this word just has a negative connotation? I mean, if you break it down, it actually makes sense. The word is "self-ish," as in having the characteristics of self. It isn't "self-all," as in *all about* self!

I thought back to all those times I did something I didn't want to do because I thought I was supposed to or because I didn't want people to get mad at me. As Heather would say, "How is that workin' out for ya, M.J.?"

I thought back to all the times when I pushed myself to do things that weren't really necessary because I felt I should, and as a result, I suffered some sort of physical, emotional, or spiritual consequence. If I had stopped for one moment in my life and thought, "Is this truly good for me? Is this going to affect me in a positive way?" and made decisions based on whether things met that criterion or not, my life would certainly be very different.

Although as I have already learned, I cannot, nor would I want to, change anything about my life. I guess what I have to think about is this: Going forward, should I embrace being this new definition of selfish, where I think about what is good for me and make decisions based on that alone? This was a head scratcher, because we all have to do stuff we don't want to do sometimes, right? Of course we do.

But it isn't about not doing things we don't want to do, it is about not doing things that are simply not good for us.

When I thought about the things I had done in the past few years that people considered selfish, such as going to California before Pete, filing for bankruptcy, not taking the bank job, and spending weeks in therapy, I saw my answer. Although those things might be considered selfish acts, they were the best things I had ever done to help move my life forward in a real, positive, sustainable way. They also were the things that helped make me a better man for those around me.

When I really thought about this version of selfish, I saw a lot of value in it. When I related it back to these people in my life who lived with this philosophy, it made even more sense. These are people who are conscientious about everything in their lives. They have the most real relationships with the people they love, the best understanding of the world and environment in which we live, and treat their bodies with a care most of us couldn't be bothered with. These are the people the outside world sees as doers and shapers of their communities. For them, all they are doing is being true to themselves and taking care of their most precious gift: themselves.

Okay, so I was a believer now, and I definitely knew that this was something I wanted to explore. I wanted to embrace this concept and be the type of person people respect and want to emulate. Getting started on this was much harder than I thought, however, because there is one underlying principle in this philosophy that is essential in making this practice work.

You have to love yourself.

To me, just thinking about that concept made me uncomfortable. I thought many things about myself, but loving myself was not one of them. I always marvel at people who really believe in and love themselves. I am aware that they probably have insecurities of some sort, but the ability to go about the world with unwavering confidence is an advantage that can take you far in life.

In a weird way, I have always had an inner confidence with some things. Although I couldn't even look in a mirror for most of my life, if you put me on a stage in front of a million people, without a note or a script or a song to sing, I would be thrilled and would hit it out of the park. I believed that I was a good person and that, if ever I was able to get my issues together, I would be capable of doing great things in this world. Having some confidence was a wonderful gift that helped me make it this far, if just barely, but it is not the same as loving yourself.

So what does it really mean to love yourself? I think that to really love yourself, it means you have to accept who you are, flaws and all, past, present, and future, and embrace it without apologies. You have to know who you are and live being content that you are exactly who you were meant to be. You also need to live in the present and enjoy it. I don't know about you, but that seems like a very hard thing to do.

I decided it was my responsibility to learn how to love this person I am, flaws and all, while still working toward being the person I want to be. I mean, isn't that the point in life? Maybe I had to continue working on myself with the tools I have gained in the past few years but with this idea of self-acceptance and self-love being my singular goal. I realized that if I could achieve this, the magnitude of this achievement would radiate more positivity to every aspect of my life and into the lives of those I love. What could be more life changing and fulfilling than that?

I knew the first step would be to stop dwelling on how much I screwed up and how much failure I have experienced while figuring out how to keep the lessons of that time close to me. I needed a better way of thinking about my past, so I came up with something that would work for me. I realized this wasn't the Lifetime movie I thought it was, it was just part of the series that had to play out. I now like to think of this part of my life and all of my past as the first few seasons of *The M.J. Show*.

Those seasons have finished taping, already have aired, and have given me the foundation for the rest of the series to continue. It is there for me to look at, reflect on, and pull lessons from whenever I need to, but not to obsess over. I can't waste time thinking about what has already taped when I need to focus on the current season filming right now.

I also started embracing my new definition of selfish in hopes that it would lead me to a bit of self-love. First and foremost, I make sure I am keeping my health a priority. I eat good foods that nourish my body and keep me satiated. I try to remember it isn't about a number on a scale or how I look, it is about giving my body everything it needs to succeed. I also stay active and remember to be careful with my joints and extremities. I want to stay in one piece as much as possible – you don't realize how important mobility is until you don't have it!

I continue to pursue a career in acting by taking classes, auditioning, and doing background work. I spend much more time than I did in the past singing, playing the guitar, and performing live when I can. Nothing in this world makes me feel more like me than music, so I follow Ricky Martin's advice and make sure I incorporate music into my life every day. I try to spend quality time with Pete, my dog Piper, and the friends and family who support me as much as possible and make me feel good. I also make it a point to be outside as much as possible, go to the beach, and basically focus on doing things that make me appreciate my surroundings. I try to remember that the things that make me happiest of all are not found in a store.

I also changed my thoughts on who I surround myself with in life. Lots of relationships can lead to a lot of work. For the people I love who tend to need a lot of attention and who can be extremely negative, the "emotional vampires," I realize that even though I love them, I can't let them be too involved in my life. By keeping them close to me, I was giving so much energy to them that I didn't have enough energy for me. I certainly didn't want to hurt anyone, because I cared about them, but I had to do what was best for me. As difficult as it was, I started distancing myself. Once I did that, I realized that if you keep your circle tight and full of supportive, positive people, your life tends to be filled with support and positivity. Imagine that!

Another important step on the road to loving yourself that I found to be imperative is forgiveness – not just for those who do wrong to you, but for yourself. FORGIVE YOURSELF for things that you do wrong, and don't be so hard on yourself. A major thing I learned is that we are all just doing the best we can on this big planet of ours with the issues we're dealing with. No one is perfect, so don't worry about trying to be.

Everyone has issues, and if someone behaves a certain way or does something to you that you don't like, you have every reason to be upset, react, or even remove them from your life. Just try to remember that even if they did do whatever it was on purpose, and it was for no other reason than to just be mean, their behavior is the result of something that happened to them at some point in their life. Just forgive them and try to let it go.

I know that there are a lot of people who are going to say all sorts of things about me when they read this book, some because they are still mad about the events that went down when I couldn't pay my bills, some because they think I have no right to succeed. Some are going to say that by writing this, I think I am better than them, and some will just say things to trash me because by trashing me, they will feel better about themselves. I know that none of those things are true, and I finally know it is something I shouldn't be worried about.

A few years ago, that would have torn me up so much, dwelling on what people would say, that I maybe wouldn't even have written the book. Now, I know that if after all these years, after I have legally settled everything needed to take care of what happened, and after acknowledging my mistakes, if people need to continue focusing on me and my life, it is less about me and my issues and more about them and their issues. If they need to do that, it is okay with me. Again, everyone is really just doing the best they can in this world with the issues they have.

Implementing these rules in my life has certainly made a difference, but to say that today I love myself would be a flat-out lie. I am still a work in progress. I do know that I understand and appreciate myself more now though than I ever have before and it is making a difference in every aspect of my life. Sure, I still make mistakes (in fact, I still make major ones), but I no longer think of them as failures. They are what they are: mistakes, and we all make them. Maybe I will never truly love myself, but as long as I am working toward that goal, then I feel like I am a success.

EPILOGUE
"Late Show"
To sum it all up.

As I started writing this book, the format changed many times. At first, I wanted to basically write a manual-type book that showed people tips and tricks for getting back on their feet in the event they screw up their life as badly as I did. I planned on glossing over the details of my story and focusing more on what happened when I bounced checks or had charges filed against me and talk about what I should have done to avoid it.

I also wanted to tell the reader to make sure they don't ignore issues that are happening in their life, and if you are in debt, keep clear communication with your creditors. I thought the lessons I learned were so basic and easy that had I known them, I would have been spared from all that happened.

I wanted to share my thoughts on how silly it is to get into debt or in trouble by trying to pursue material things. I planned on sharing stories like how I dealt with people mocking me for having a flip phone on movie sets in Los Angeles, wearing thrift-store clothes, or even because I took the bus. I did handle these situations well and learned from them the value of living within your means.

While I was writing that version of the book, I began to understand that these were really not the life lessons that mattered. Although I really loved some of my chapter titles, such as "Bouncing is more fun on a trampoline!" and "Buy K-mart, not Kardashian," I knew that the important things I learned along the way were the things I wasn't planning on learning. Knowing what to do when your car is getting repossessed won't change your life! It may help at the time, but it won't make the same lasting impact as learning some of the other lessons I learned.

So I scrapped that whole manuscript and started fresh with this one. I knew I needed to tell every intimate detail of my life and my failures so people could believe my words. I wanted to establish credibility in hope that people would actually see that I really may have learned a thing or two. I hope people can see how quickly life can change and how you can go from failure and despair to hope and happiness by just taking one step at a time.

I no longer feel like a total failure. I consider myself a reformed failure, or a failure in recovery. I know that I am not a noun but a verb and am constantly changing and growing. From examining my life, working through a lot of pain, and wanting, more than anything, to live a happy life, I have learned a few things, and I hope I can continue to share all I have learned with people who need support.

So if you feel like you need the CliffsNotes version of these lessons I have learned along the way, then I present to you:

M.J.'s Top Ten Life Lessons from a Total Failure (Did I mention that if I wasn't on a sitcom, I would love to be a talk show host?)

10. If you are unhappy with your life, change it. No matter who you are, where you are, or what your circumstances are, if you are unhappy in your life, do something to make it better. Whether you believe it or not, you always have at least two options in life: you can either accept things the way they are or change them. The choice is always there. It may not be easy, it may not be fun, but anyone, anywhere, at any stage of their life, can wipe the slate clean and move forward being the person that truly reflects on the outside, who they are on the inside.

9. Time is precious; don't waste it. I realize how much time I wasted being upset about so much that I couldn't control. I let a lot of time slip through my fingers, and I let a lot of opportunities go by me. Stop waiting for certain criteria to be met to start living your life and just start living. You really never know how much time you have, and not one day is worth wasting.

8. Don't let your emotions control you. Never let the highs get too high or the lows get to low. Having balance, or "middle ground" as Uncle Jerry says, helps you live a life that is consistent and stable. You will still be able to feel and experience all that you should in life, but you will never tip the scale to one extreme or the other. And once the scale is tipped in either direction, it takes work to get back to stability.

7. Follow your passions. Your passions are what make you unique. They are the essence of who you are. If you don't pursue and share them, how will you ever be fulfilled? How will the world around you ever know what makes you special? Whether you call them passions, dreams, hopes, or desires, don't be satisfied with not working toward having them in your life.

6. Relationships are earned, not required. No one person in your life has a free pass to stay there. No matter what the relationship, you don't need to keep people around you who don't respect, love, support, or encourage you. Stop wasting energy with these people, and put that energy into the relationships of those who truly do care about you. Cultivating those relationships will bring you more joy in life and far less stress.

5. Recognize and appreciate the good things in your life. Whether it is a person who you often remind of how special they are to you or the car you are so thankful to have that you make sure it is clean and taken care of at all times. Be grateful for all blessings you have in life.

4. Looking to others for validation is a fool's errand.

No matter how long or hard you look, no external validation will ever give you peace. Work on being a whole person, and you will attract people and things to your life that make you content.

3. Always remember to forgive yourself and others. It is a good practice that will heal you and those around you. Don't expect perfection from yourself or others, either, or you will never be anything but disappointed.

2. Permit yourself to be my definition of selfish. Make your mental, spiritual, and physical health paramount. You only have one body and one life. Without your health, you have nothing. Treat yourself like you would treat your most valued loved one. Remember that if you don't take care of yourself, you won't be well enough to take care of others.

And the most important life lesson I have learned from my failures is...

1. Learn to love yourself. Nothing is more important, and nothing will make your life more worthwhile than remembering this. The more you work on you, the more you will become the person you are meant to be, and the more you will make a lasting impact on the world and those you love.

I am not sure how many seasons of my show I will get to play out, but I know that I am going to put my all into every episode, every day. I will work hard to be the man I want to be, maintain and nurture the relationships that are dear to me, and make my passions a part of my daily routine. Who knows, maybe one day you will be flipping through your TV channels, and you will see a new series starring a lovable and zany guy who is a recovering total failure. When you do, make sure to watch for the opening and theme song... I have been planning that in my head for over thirty years!

ACKNOWLEDGMENTS
"The Credits"

Writing a book is a long and often tedious process that does not happen without the patience, support, and love of those around you. Although this was my story, it involved many other people and I appreciate the time everyone took to talk to me about each detail of this time period as I tried to make sure every line of this book is as accurately portrayed as possible. So many people supported me along this journey that I would have to add a whole chapter to thank them all, but for those of you who supported me so fully, and you know who you are, I thank you.

ABOUT THE AUTHOR

M.J. Dougherty is a recovering failure originally from the adorable town of Clarks Summit, PA. *Life Lessons from a Total Failure* is M.J.'s first book and he is keeping his fingers crossed that readers won't hope it will be his last. M.J. can frequently be found talking to others about the events of his life and helping motivate them toward the life of their dreams. When he's not sharing his disasters with the world and helping them get back on track, M.J. can be found either on the set of one of your favorite television shows, singing wherever anyone will listen, or enjoying his life in Los Angeles, CA.

For more information go to www.mjdougherty.com.